MORE THAN MOUNTAINS

THE TODD HUSTON STORY

One Leg, *Russell,*

Fifty *See you at the top!*

Mountains, *Todd H*

An

Unconquerable

Faith

Todd Huston, Julie Dunbar, & Kay Rizzo

Edited by Dodie Preston
Cover design by Ed Guthero, Dodie Preston
Cover photo by Dan Miller

Dedication

To those who want to stand on top.

Thanks

To reach the top of my mountains, I was assisted by the efforts of many. I thank God for these people.

My family, who was a source of strength, encouragement, and laughter;
Lisa, who worked hard and kept the faith;
Whit, for being there and sticking it out;
Our sponsors – John Shanahan of Hooked on Phonics, Flex-Foot, and the individuals who believed in and supported my dream;
Ron Gladden, for getting the word out;
Everyone who prayed for us – it really works.

Contents

Contents

Forward

The beauty from atop a mountain can be a very spiritual experience, and very symbolic of our life journey. We all have greatness within us – it is how we are created. Eventually we live that greatness, and it is the most brilliant light we could ever imagine. It beams through all of the darkness, not only in our lives, but the lives of those with whom we come into contact, and even those upon whom our thoughts rest. Getting to that point can seem like quite a hike up a strenuous mountain because, throughout our journey, we cram our packs full of dark and unnecessary debris. This debris may take the form of impatience, anger, or greed. It may take the form of a negative self-image. It could take the form of addiction, abuse, or illegal activities. Its aim is to cast a shadow over us and dim our light; however, it only has the power we give it. We can make the choice to unload our pack of this vile debris and toss it to the wind. The more we unload, the easier becomes our ascent, until we let go of every false suggestion of who we are and recognize our true, beautiful identity, pure and untouched. At this moment we look up and pause, realizing with bated breath we have reached our summit. All around us is a view words fail to capture – incredible beauty, freedom, joy, love, and peace, all in abundance. As we silently stand on the top of our mountain, a familiarity slowly dawns within us. We realize the summit was never a destination; we've been there all along, we simply needed to let go of the darkness to see it.

May this, and other of Todd's works, help you to stand atop your summit and experience the amazing view.

Julie Dunbar

CHAPTER ONE

Foot of Denali

Man is not ready for adventure unless he is rid of fear.

For fear confines him and limits his scope. He stays tethered by strings of

doubt and indecision and has only a small and narrow world to explore.

(William O. Douglas, Of Men and Mountains [New York: Harper and Brothers Publisher, 1950], x)

"I can't feel my legs." I shout ahead into the storm not knowing if anyone can hear me. I'm almost 17,000 feet up one of the most deadly mountains in the world and I'm as blind as a bat and bitterly cold. The blazing whiteness of the Bering Sea blizzard is worse than any darkness I have ever experienced, and it is blowing my consciousness into confusion. I have to maintain my concentration or I'm a dead man.

This is the mountain; the unforgiving fortress that brings life to the soul, but can kill the body. It makes no distinction as man's world does; no delineation based on culture, race, gender, or disability. You are at its mercy and it makes no exceptions. It is the judge and jury, and I realize with dread it has yet to decide my fate. As a leg amputee, many think my "Summit America" expedition is bordering on insanity, and as I reach to assemble every bit of faith and energy I possess, I realize the mountain probably agrees.

I inch my way up the ridge. I can barely make out the sound of my steel crampons over the wailing wind as they scrape against the rocks. My right crampon begins twisting to the side as my left one balls up with snow, making traction nearly impossible. These razor sharp additions to my boots can't cut into the resisting ice. The Eskimos have named this type of ice "tugartaq." It is hard and slippery and is a climber's worst enemy. I

1

yearn to prove that within me lies an enormous strength more powerful than any challenge I face, and with stern resolve I determine this is one battle the mountain isn't going to win.

Mount McKinley, or as the locals and climbers refer to it, Denali. In a land crisscrossed by mountain ranges that make Colorado fourteeners look like anthills, there is no mistaking this mountain is different. If you don't know how dangerous it is, all you have to do is look at the awe, respect, and fear on the faces of those who dare attempt its summit.

Sitting one hundred thirty-five miles north of Anchorage, Denali shoulders its way above the neighboring peaks at a majestic elevation of 20,320 feet. It is only three-and-a-half degrees south of the Arctic Circle, making it 2,400 miles farther north than Everest.

This granite monolith, with moods both capricious and unforgiving, wears a perpetual shroud of snow and ice. It is considered by some to be the toughest mountain in the world to conquer. The climb from base camp to the summit is 13,120 feet. This is over 1,500 feet higher than the climb up Mount Everest.

Furthermore, temperatures can plummet down to minus one hundred degrees Fahrenheit, while storms can gust up to one hundred fifty miles per hour.

In 1896, William A. Dickey, a Princeton graduate who struck gold in the Yukon, named Mount McKinley after former Senator, and later U.S. President, William McKinley. The native Athabascans call the mountain Denali. Other natives refer to it as Traleika. Showing more wisdom than the Ivy-league explorers, their names delineate it as the Great One.

I've never seen fault in those who would like to get the name changed back to Denali. Climbers call the mountain Denali out of respect. [*]

Many venture to climb it each year, but few have much success. Even those wanting to view the summit from its base typically find it prefers to stay hidden under a blanket of clouds.

Bart, our taxi driver from Anchorage to Talkeetna, talked about how magnificent the mountain looks on a clear day. "But those days are rare," he added.

---

[*] The name was officially changed to Denali in 2015

I should have realized those clouds do nothing but wrap climbers in cold and wet. What was I thinking when I eagerly loaded our gear into that wreck of a yellow station wagon?

"I guess you'll be up there soon," said Bart. I sensed he knew we may not all come back. The fact is these taxis take more climbers to the mountain than they bring home.

After spitting out the window, Bart bellowed, "Last month I drove a group of would-be climbers up here. It was a beautiful clear day. They got out of the car, looked at the mountain, said, 'No way,' got back in the car, and went back to Anchorage."

With those encouraging words, Bart dropped Adrian, Mike, Whit, and I in front of Doug Keating's Bunkhouse, where we arranged to get a good night's sleep before starting our climb.

The bunkhouse was a charming log chateau set off the main road in Talkeetna. I was surprised by the number of people I saw walking in and out of the restaurants, saloons, and bunkhouses in this old Alaskan village.

I studied the faces of the people and could instantly tell who had yet to attempt the mountain and who had just returned. Those getting ready to climb it were eager to conquer the challenge that lay ahead. They excitedly talked about the route they would take, bragged about other mountains they'd climbed, and boldly exclaimed how anxious they were to bag this one.

Then there were the ones who looked as though they'd been in the midst of a fierce battle. They didn't talk about how they won or lost on the mountain, they were only glad to be back. Their slow gait, faces of tanned leather, and eyes battered by fatigue told the story. No bragging, just respect for the Great One.

I didn't know what my face said, but inside I had a feeling it was possible I wouldn't make it off Denali alive.

I stopped a man wearing North Face climbing pants and a matching fleece jacket and introduced myself. A moment of small talk about where we were from led to questions about the climb.

"Are there always this many climbers hanging around?" I asked.

He smiled. "Haven't you heard about the weather? No one is going to, or leaving from, the mountain until these storms pass."

I looked toward the direction of the mountain and saw the impenetrable storm clouds, brooding and ponderous, daring any air taxi to come through.

"Do you think there will be a problem getting up to the glacier tomorrow?" I continued.

The climber shrugged. "Don't know. This mountain makes its own weather, and the pilots need a break in the clouds to get through." I wished him the best on getting to the summit and headed to my bunkhouse.

Its interior lacked the charm of the exterior. It was one big noisy room with a loft, and was cluttered with backpacks, gear, food sacks, sleeping bags, trash, and climbers.

In the middle of it sat my expedition guide, Adrian Crane, who was perched atop our gear heap. We brought everything we'd used throughout our entire expedition thus far, but didn't need all of it for this climb. It was crucial to travel as lightly as possible, so Adrian was separating everything out.

Adrian was more than just another climber. He was the current U.S. State highpoints record holder. He climbed to the highest point in each of the fifty states in a record one hundred one days.

I followed our lead climber, Mike, through the noisy maze, dismally realizing my dream of getting a good night's sleep was unlikely.

I crawled into my sleeping bag and rolled away from the light streaming through the windows, but the crowd of climbers talking and stepping over me made sleep futile. I wasn't sure how I'd get any rest, and I desperately needed it before we got to the glacier.

"Ready to eat?" Whit never met a meal he didn't like. I looked up at his smiling face as he smacked on gorp – a trail mix made with peanuts, raisins, and M&M's. I was tired and over-anxious, but I was also hungry. I decided I might as well get up and eat, considering my hunger was the only thing I seemed to have any control over at the time.

The four of us walked across the street to McKinley Deli. I tried to downplay my anxiety in front of the others, but it was to no avail. I was really getting scared.

"So, what will you boys have?" a burly short-order cook with a thick and wild beard asked as he flipped burgers on the grill. "We have the best

4

burgers in town."

More appropriately, the only burgers.

We ordered a couple of sandwiches and some pizza, then headed for one of the empty picnic tables.

We were barely seated when a couple of climbers dragged themselves through the doors. By the exhaustion on their sunburned faces, and the painful way they moved, I could tell they'd just come down. I was curious about what I was getting myself into and knew they would be a great source of information. It still wasn't too late to back out.

"What's it like up there?" I asked.

One of the men shook his head. "Bad storms and high winds. We were locked in at Denali Pass for three days."

Realizing how close they were to the summit I asked, "But did you summit?"

Again he shook his head. "No. Somehow, the summit loses its significance in the face of survival." He probably saw me as a neophyte who didn't know how to make a good judgment call on the mountain.

He downed some more cider and continued, "I'm just happy to get off that mountain alive. I'm definitely ready to go home, and glad it's not in a body-bag."

They came all the way to Alaska, spent thousands of dollars, were that close to the summit, and didn't make it? I stared incredulously. How disappointing.

Here I was, a relatively inexperienced climber, hearing how the seasoned climbers feared for their lives.

He excused himself to place a phone call. "My wife's going to be so glad to hear I'm on my way home."

His climbing buddy stared into his hot cup as if still trying to ward off the chill from the storm.

"Really bad, huh?" I asked.

"It's an experience I'll never forget." He stared at me with a haunted expression in his eyes, as if measuring his words by my reactions. "At 19,000 feet, I chiseled a step into the ice and found a climber's glove. When I went to grab the glove, I realized the climber's hand was still in it."

5

A shiver of fear coursed down my spine. That was not what I needed to hear to cure my anxiety. "A human hand?" I asked, as if any other hand could be wearing a glove.

"By the style of the glove, I suspect I came across a climber lost on the mountain in the early seventies. All those years, locked in ice." He didn't have that cocky look about him I assumed he had before he started his climb. He shook his head. "I consider myself a very good climber with a lot of experience. But right now, I feel very lucky to be down here, safe and alive."

"I'm a dead man," I whispered to myself as I stared down at the hot slice of pepperoni pizza on the table before me. "I'm really dead."

I'd never been so scared in my life.

Not during or after the boating accident.

Not even before my leg amputation.

I must have been crazy for thinking I could climb Denali.

CHAPTER TWO

Tragedy at Tenkiller

"Help me! Stop! Help me!" I screamed as loudly as I could while choking on the warm Lake Tenkiller water. "Stop the boat!" Tangled in the ski rope, I bobbed helplessly in the water while watching the boat drift back toward me. The sound of churning water being expelled by the eighteen-inch propellers was getting dangerously close. I quickly looked around for an escape route through the maze of ski rope entangling me. The life jacket prevented me from being able to move quickly and I seemed unable to swim away from the rotating jaws inching my way. I recalled the strange feeling I had before getting onto the boat that day, as though something dark was going to happen.

I glanced about wildly for a way out. I needed help but there wasn't any. Despite having six people on the boat, my screams were going unheard. Inside the boat my family and friends were laughing and talking, totally unaware the engine had slipped into reverse and was drifting back in a direct path toward me. I was seized with terror. I had to get out of there!

I ducked under the rope and flailed frantically at the water, but the more I fought the more the web held me. The life vest prevented me from swimming under the rope and the noise of the engine was becoming deafening. Everything seemed to be in slow motion, as though I was in a nightmare fighting against an irresistible force. I continued with all of my strength to free myself from impending doom.

Behind me I heard the gurgling noise of the boat as it practically rested on my shoulders. I felt a bump, then my legs began to be sucked under the water. I flailed my arms wildly to keep my head above it. The boat propellers began crawling up my legs, tossing me back and forth like a puppy chewing on a rag doll. The one hundred eighty-eight horsepower inboard/outboard engine with a propeller nearly the size of my waist was determining my destiny. I squeezed my eyes shut and fought the death grip holding me. There was no escaping as the blade sliced its way up my legs like hamburger through a meat grinder. If only this were just a bad dream.

The boat stopped to a grinding halt.

I opened my eyes. Silvery specks burst across the sky. The dark green Oklahoma lake water was now stained dark red. "Ahh!" I wailed, thrashing about in an ever-widening circle of blood.

Despite all the chaos, I heard a calm voice. It was as if time no longer existed and I was removed from the moment. Was it my imagination or was it real? It seemed very real. I heard a soft voice telling me I had a choice. "You can come home now or stay. If you choose to stay it will be a very hard fight."

Somewhere deep in my being I made the choice to stay.

I felt my father's hand grab my life jacket from the shoulder and immediately I was pulled out of the water. As I was being lifted into the air above the back of the boat I saw my legs, and began screaming, "Why me! Why me!" At the young age of fourteen, my life had dramatically changed.

I thrashed around as blood spurted out four to six feet in a pulsating fountain from a sliced femoral artery. Like a runaway garden hose, it was spraying my father, the face of my friend, Clay Bird, and everything and everybody else in its range. I had never seen so much blood in my life.

My father placed me on the floor of the boat and I was soon laying in a pool of my own blood. This was when I saw the full extent of my injuries.

My left thigh was open to the bone, my muscles were exposed, and my skin was flapped open. My father quickly threw a towel over the red and purple muscles saturated in blood. The backside of my right leg was missing, except for shreds of dangling, stringy tissue.

As I tried to squirm I noticed my right foot would not move. "Dad, I can't move my foot!"

Pressing the towel hard on my leg, he responded, "Calm down, Todd. Try not to move. Clay, help me here."

Clay gaped at me, his face pale as a ghost and his eyes wide with fright. "Clay! Come on, give me some help here!" My dad then grabbed Clay's hands and pressed them against the towel behind my right leg. "Hold on and press hard against his leg." Clay reluctantly grabbed on tight.

I looked to the front of the boat and saw my friend Brook Baxter thrusting her head forward as she vomited over the side. When Emily Shepherd, another of my friends, saw what happened, she held my four-year-old brother, Stevie, and covered his eyes. He was screaming as she escorted him to the front of the boat.

The excruciating pain was throwing my body into contortions as I lay in the bottom of the boat, smashed up against the sidewall between the middle and back seats. My twelve-year-old brother, Scott, just starred with a ghastly look on his face. With nowhere to get away, everyone was trapped in nightmarish terror.

"Scott!" My father reached for another beach towel to cover the blood soaked ones on my leg. "Get up there and drive!"

Scott shook his head in panic. "I can't! I don't know how!"

"You have to! We have got to get this bleeding stopped before it is too late!"

Too late for what? I saw the crimson towels and again tried to move my right foot.

"Hold on, Todd. We're going to get you to a doctor." My dad reached up and started the boat and moved the throttle forward.

The engine coughed to a start, then sputtered to life. I could feel the vibration and smell the gas as I lay near the engine compartment. Suddenly, the boat lurched forward with its nose in the air and began speeding across the water.

"Scott, grab the wheel and head in that direction," my dad directed. I could hear the boat growling its way to shore as he pointed it toward Elk Landing several miles across the lake.

I squinted at the late afternoon sun. The specks of light pelted my eyes. Dizzy from the pain and the loss of so much blood, I writhed about on the floor of the boat. I could hear my father shouting to Clay to keep holding down tight on the pressure points as the blood continued to seep into the boat.

"Why me?" I kept asking myself as my father continued throwing one towel onto another, then wringing the blood out to use the same towels over again.

I moved my gaze from my mangled left leg to my right leg. Ignoring the lacerations and split-open kneecap, I tried again to move my foot. Why wouldn't it move? I kept telling my dad, "It won't move, I can't get my foot to move!"

My father tried to reassure me, "It's OK, Todd. We're going to get you to a doctor and get you fixed in no time."

My years of Cub and Boy Scout training penetrated my curtain of pain. I remembered the instructions we received if we found ourselves in an emergency. Remain calm and don't panic.

I clinched my teeth together to keep them from chattering and began telling myself, "Remain calm. Remain calm."

For a time, I concentrated on trying to move my foot, but it wouldn't move. During the fifteen-minute ride back to the boat dock, I lost track of time. Thoughts popped in and out of my mind regarding school, football, and my friends.

I tried to use conversation to help calm the situation. "Do you think I will be ready to play football next month?" Clay and I played on the starting football team, and Emily and Brook were both cheerleaders. "Will I have to sit on the bench?" They tried to politely assure me I would be on the team this year, again as the starting linebacker.

Wham! Suddenly the boat hit the dock and the nose went up, violently tilting to the right. I could hear the screech as the side of the boat slid along the dock, bringing it to a stop.

"Are we here?" I asked.

Without answering, my father stood up and shouted to the people on the dock, "Call an ambulance. My son's been injured. I can't stop the bleeding!"

I glanced down at the blood I had been lying in, my own blood, and in a barely audible voice cried, "Oh God, help me."

A stranger pushed through the crowd of gawking spectators, "I'm a doctor. Let me help you with him." He helped my dad lift me out of the boat onto the dock.

Then a woman approached. "Can I help? I'm a nurse." She didn't wait for a reply and quickly rushed to assist the physician.

At the time it didn't occur to me that it was a small miracle a physician and nurse, who didn't even know each other, happened to be in such a remote location exactly when I needed them. Looking back, I know it wasn't chance.

"I'm thirsty," I moaned. "I need something to drink." My tongue felt swollen and dry in the hot July afternoon.

The doctor shouted orders as he worked over my body, "Get him some ice to suck on." Someone stuck a couple of ice chips on my tongue, and told me it was all I could have right now.

My friend Emily sat near me and said, "Todd, don't forget how tough you are."

"Get me towels, anything you have I can use to wrap his legs," the doctor shouted. Then turning to me he asked, "How are you feeling Todd?" He seemed to be in his environment.

The onlookers continued to stare, some with concern, others with curiosity.

I nodded as a suffocating blanket of pain smothered my awareness of everything but the pain and thirst. I'd always heard when someone is severely injured their body shuts down and they don't feel the pain. Not true!

I fought against the intense numbness threatening to engulf me, to swallow up my consciousness. Then, from somewhere distant, I heard the wail of an ambulance siren.

I hoped the ambulance would have something to help ease the intensity of the pain, but when the emergency vehicle careened to a stop at the edge of the wooden pier, and the white-jacketed paramedics burst from the vehicle, no one was listening to my requests for pain medication.

I kept trying to reassure myself, "All I need is a few stitches and something for the pain and I'll be fine."

They were intent on getting me to the hospital as quickly as possible.

As they were loading me onto the stretcher I screamed in agony. People continued gawking. Years later I learned the nurse thought I was probably a goner. My dad took my hand with his distraught face looming over me, his eyes filled with concern.

"Dad," I tried to smile, but could only manage to wince, "what's going to happen to me?"

He replied something, but I was unable to discern his words.

The stretcher collapsed and I found myself inside the ambulance.

"Go! Go! Go!" yelled the paramedic to the driver.

I heard the ambulance peel away from the dock, spewing a shower of gravel and dust in its wake.

I looked around and saw tubes, bottles, and lots of stuff packaged in paper. The doctor continued to take my vital signs and relay them to the paramedics, who radioed them ahead to the hospital.

"Please give me something for the pain." No one seemed to hear me over the siren, or else they were ignoring me. All I could do was clench my father's hand and tightly hold onto the bar of the stretcher.

The ambulance sped along the twisty country roads of the Cookson Hills toward the small town of Tahlequah, some twenty minutes from the lake.

It screeched to a halt and the back doors of the vehicle flew open. My head flopped to one side and I saw the blood that had come through the sheets.

As the attendants rolled the stretcher out and wheeled me through the automatic doors into the emergency room, I thought they might finally give me something for the pain.

Immediately, the doctor who accompanied us from the lake shouted orders at the hospital personnel.

In the flurry of nurses wrapping my legs in bandages and sticking my arm with a needle to begin an IV, I tried to be heard, "It hurts. It really hurts."

When no one responded to my request, I begged for water. I was so thirsty, my tongue was sticking to the roof of my mouth. A nurse heard my request. "We can't give you a drink, but maybe some ice will help." This sounded absurd to me.

"Mr. Huston, you were lucky that doctor was at the lake today," the physician on duty in the emergency room told my father. I strained to hear what he had to say. "Without his emergency care…well, you were just lucky, sir."

"Thank God," my father whispered.

"But your son isn't out of the woods yet. Our hospital lacks the facilities to handle this type of emergency. Todd needs attention far above our capabilities. We are going to immediately transport him to Muskogee General. We will stabilize him the best we can before he leaves, and a doctor will be on the ambulance with the two of you."

"Muskogee?" My dad echoed his words, probably wondering if the risk of moving me away from this hospital to a distant one was worth it.

"Your luck is still holding though. I just talked with Muskogee General, and it seems the hospital's surgical team was preparing to do surgery on another patient, so they are ready and waiting for Todd."

I didn't hear any more of what they talked about as I was being prepared to be rushed back to the ambulance.

The same two paramedics who carried me into the hospital lifted my stretcher and quickly wheeled me out of the emergency room exit. The ceiling lights passed above me in a blur as they ran alongside me, holding glass bottles tethered to my arm. I felt lightheaded.

A strange cold began to build in my body, as if being frozen from the inside out. My teeth were chattering, but it was over ninety degrees outside. Why was I so cold?

Along with being cold, I wanted to sleep. If I could sleep, maybe my pain would go away, for just a little while. I still hadn't received any pain medication. I was so tired. Too tired to fight. I closed my eyes as they rolled my stretcher into the ambulance.

My father climbed in behind me. He squeezed my shoulder reassuringly. "Hold on, son. We're going to Muskogee. They're sending you some blood from Tulsa and it will be there waiting for you. Everything's going to . . ."

"I'm so cold," I mumbled. It was so hard to keep my eyes open.

"What? What Todd? What did you say?"

I repeated myself with what little energy I had. "I'm c-cold." I could barely speak above a whisper. Either my father or the doctor must have figured out what I was saying, probably from my shivering, because I felt the weight of additional blankets. It was better, but I was still freezing. As the ambulance raced toward Muskogee, I tried to keep a conversation going, but it was too difficult as I slipped in and out of consciousness.

Again, I licked my parched lips, feeling so thirsty. The doctor kept dipping his hand into a Styrofoam cup and scraping out some ice for me.

Pain continued to shoot through my body. I was irritated with the paramedic who seemed to be constantly poking and prodding and shifting my body, keeping me from going to sleep.

The ambulance screeched to a halt outside Muskogee General Hospital. The door immediately swung open and a team of orderlies hauled the stretcher from the vehicle. I found myself surrounded by a horde of news reporters and photographers.

My father leaped from the back and shouted, "No pictures! No pictures!" pushing and breaking the pathway toward the hospital entrance.

Once again, I screamed in pain as they transferred me onto the emergency room table. Looking up at the clock, I realized it was almost 7:00 p.m. It had been about three hours since the boat hit me.

I continued to scream and groan as they unwrapped the bandages put on my legs in Tahlequah. I was being twisted, turned, examined, and stuck, which intensified the pain to an unbearable degree. I again felt myself going in and out of consciousness.

Somewhere between the ambulance and the examination room, I lost track of my dad and the doctor who had been with me since the dock. I was alone. Even with a swarm of people surrounding me and doing everything they could, I still felt very alone.

Shifting me to the gurney, they wheeled me to radiology and lifted me onto a cold, hard metal table. When they lifted my legs to place the steel X-ray plates beneath them, I could see the muscle from the back of my leg hanging down.

I shrieked from the intense pain. "It hurts. It hurts too much! Please stop the pain!"

"Soon, Todd," one of the nurses assured me as she told her assistant to hurry with the X-ray. Then whispered, "They almost lost him once."

I tossed back and forth trying to fight the pain.

After what seemed like an eternity, they wheeled me into an elevator. The lights dropped on the wall to a lower level. The elevator stopped and the doors slid open. They wheeled me down a hallway through another set of doors and into a pea-green tiled room. Clanging instruments and machines moved past me. I glanced around at all the knobs, gauges, and switches, and was taken aback by the sterile, operating room smell.

Masked people lifted me onto the table, holding firmly to the sheet beneath me. The room swarmed with nurses and doctors scurrying about, performing a variety of tasks. Above me was a blinding light.

I heard two male voices discussing whether or not to amputate a leg. A slight man with kind blue eyes stood behind my head, talking to me, telling me to count backward from one hundred. He placed a mask over my mouth and nose. A warm, tingling sensation began to fill my head. The pain was gone… I felt nothing at all.

I awoke in the middle of the night in the Intensive Care Unit. The tube carrying oxygen up my nose felt like a hair dryer blowing into it.

"It's all right, Todd." My mom was sitting next to me. She told me I was in the hospital and not to move too much.

She had been waiting on shore for us and wondered why we were late. Little did she know that the siren she heard was for her son.

I had to think for a moment about what had happened. I glanced at the tubes going everywhere: in my nose, in my arms, and out my legs. Different bags were around me, some filled with fluids going into me, and others with fluids coming out of me.

I reached down through all of the tubes and felt both of my legs. A wave of relief swept over me. I still had my legs.

CHAPTER THREE

Hope and Disappointment

Sleep is illusive in the bunkhouse. Between the chatter and bustle of the other climbers and my anxiety about what lay ahead, I can't seem to relax enough to let myself doze off.

I'm especially alert when an experienced climber chimes in, "The worst thing a climber can do is push himself beyond his endurance. Slow and easy is the key to success. And on this mountain, the definition of success is not summiting, it's merely coming down alive."

Who am I kidding? Can a man with only one leg really survive a Denali climb? What am I trying to prove, and is it worth the cost? How hard can I push myself without risking my life, or endangering the success of the expedition?

Then I remember I've spent the last twenty years pushing myself against impossible odds – since the day my legs were ripped to shreds by the boat propeller.

Sleep eluded me throughout the days after the accident. I was under the impression that rest was important for the healing process, but there was a constant barrage of hospital staff taking my vital signs, bringing me meds, wheeling me to get X-rayed, and drawing my blood. While lying peacefully on the bed, I would feel a pull on my arm or see a light shining in my face. I decided if a person wanted rest, they needed to stay away from hospitals.

I vaguely remembered my parents coming and going from Intensive Care over the next few days. The doctors who'd used their skills to save my life and legs came by regularly. Loaded with pain medications, it felt like I was in a dream when I heard the snippets of information they told my parents.

"Lost three-fourths of his blood…"

"He flat-lined on us twice…"

"Not enough skin on his right leg to close the wound."

"We seriously considered amputating the right leg."

"One lucky guy."

"God must have been with him."

When I fully regained consciousness, my mother was sitting on a chair crammed between the wall and the bed. It had to be hard for her because she was eight-and-a-half months pregnant.

I saw a newspaper protruding from her purse, which was resting on the bedside table. It hurt to move my fingers because of the needles implanted in the back of my hand, but I was able to lift the paper so I could read it. There, on the front page, was an article about me.

I started to laugh. What was this? "…is in critical condition at Muskogee Hospital." I was hurt and sore, but I didn't feel critical. I didn't realize how much of my comfort was due to the pain medications, not my well-being.

"How many days until I go home, mom?" I asked.

"We'll just have to wait and see. The doctors are doing everything they can to help you get home soon," she lovingly replied.

Then I remembered my foot. I still could not move my right foot. "Mom, what's wrong with my foot? I can't move it."

"The doctor said it may take some time to heal." I think she was hoping for a miracle, because the truth was seven inches of my sciatic nerve, the nerve that moves your foot, was chopped out by the boat propeller.

After a week in ICU they moved me to a regular room. I was hoping to get away from the constant monitoring and get some sleep. Instead I was placed in a room with a guy who'd just had hernia surgery and was constantly groaning.

A bar running overhead the length of my bed blocked my view of the TV, so I spent a lot of time thinking while looking up at the ceiling tiles.

The question that kept coming was, "Why me, God? Why did this have to happen to me?" I didn't have any control over my life or body. Everyone but me seemed to be deciding my fate.

The worst visits were from the nurses who were on the early shift. Every morning they woke me up to draw more blood. Hadn't I lost enough already?

But it wasn't all bad. In spite of my discomfort, I enjoyed the attention I was receiving. Complete strangers sent me letters and cards letting me know they were praying for me. Church members came to visit. My friends came down from Tulsa in groups, bringing all kinds of gifts. I felt like a celebrity.

Actually, I didn't know how I would have made it without my friends. They really helped ease the pain.

DeAnn, a cheerleader, and Emily, who'd been with me at the lake, were really sweet and made me laugh. My friend Mike came to visit whenever he could. He told me the latest news about my buddies, but hesitated when I asked him about football.

Football was my life. As middle linebacker I held the record for the most team tackles during the seventh and eighth grades. I was eager to get back into the game, especially with the season getting ready to begin. Of course, first I needed to be able to get out of bed.

Ten days after the accident, my mother gave birth to my little sister at a Tulsa hospital. The week after her delivery seemed interminable to me because she wasn't able to visit until her doctor gave her permission to make the fifty-mile drive to Muskogee. Fortunately, Dr. Miller, a friend of my grandparents who lived near Lake Tenkiller, stayed with me while my parents were in Tulsa. He sat and talked with me for hours while I chewed the Trident gum he brought.

It was hard not to notice the pungent rotten egg smell from the green ooze seeping through my bandages. There was a lot of bacteria in the lake water so my leg became infected with Pseudomonas. Every other day the orderlies would wheel me into the operating room, anesthetize me, and change my bandages. I would be in immense pain the entire next day, and would only begin to feel better when it was time for them to do it all over again.

One day they attempted to change my bandages without sedating me. As I lay on my belly and they lifted the first layer of gauze off the raw flesh on the back of my leg, a searing pain shot through me, far worse than what I'd endured immediately after the accident. All I could do was scream. It was so ear-piercingly loud that other staff members in the hospital came running to find out what was happening. We went back to the sedation routine.

After a few weeks I began to realize I might not be back at school in time to play football for the ninth grade season. What I didn't know was the surgeons had told my parents my leg was going to be permanently paralyzed, and I would probably never walk again.

I was wasting away in the hospital when I should have been getting stronger. My body was shrinking from lying in bed. I was healing, but in the world I was used to, I was becoming weak and ineffective.

"God, why?" I prayed for instant miracles and answers, but they would not come. Was God listening? I joked with Him that patience wasn't my greatest virtue, so I would appreciate a little expedience with all of this. However, I knew this was no laughing matter.

I learned to improvise to keep myself from losing any more muscle mass. The most I could do was work on my arms. I used the pull-up bar over my head which was there to help me shift my body. After each set of ten pull-ups I flopped back against my pillow and caught my breath. I remembered how Clay and I used to flex our muscles in front of the mirror after lifting weights together. We were so cocky. I now looked with disgust at my emaciated body.

Then, one day, I finally heard the words that were music to my ears, "OK Todd. It's time to get up." I'd waited a long time for this day. The last steps I'd taken were when I jumped off the boat to go inner-tubing.

The nurse sat me up on the edge of the bed. "Whoa!" Everything in the room started spinning.

"That's normal after lying in bed for as long as you have."

When I couldn't fight the dizziness any longer I laid back down. I reminded myself this didn't mean I had failed. I knew this was just one step toward my recovery, and it was going to take one step at a time to heal. I continued sitting up until the spinning stopped.

It was time to try again. The nurse insisted I use a walker.

"I'm not some old man," I touted, as I gripped the bars and tried to stand. "Whoa!" I couldn't believe how much my legs felt like noodles. I couldn't control them and they didn't provide any stability. Even worse, I could feel the blood rushing down my legs creating immense internal pressure on my wounds. It hurt so badly!

I immediately sat back on the bed. This was not going to be easy.

19

The nurse put the walker in the corner and said she would return the next day. She said consolingly, "You did great!"

Who was she kidding? Maybe I did do great, but it sure didn't feel that way.

Over the next couple of weeks, I moved from the bed to a wheelchair, from a wheelchair to crutches, and from crutches to walking with the aid of an ugly metal brace which kept my paralyzed right foot from drooping.

The best part was I was finally at the stage where the doctors felt comfortable discharging me.

This left me with such mixed emotions. I was happy to be going home, but I knew I would miss all of the new friends I'd made who'd taken such good care of me.

My dad, my football coach, and my friend Mike picked me up for my ceremonial drive home.

"You excited to be getting back to your friends and family?" Coach Smiley asked as we drove toward Tulsa.

"Yes!" I replied vehemently, while stretched out in the back of his station wagon which was padded with pillows. Though it was reminiscent of my ambulance ride to the hospital, this was the one ride I'd eagerly anticipated for six weeks. I was so excited to be going home my stomach was doing flips.

When we pulled up in front of my house, I saw ribbons, balloons, and banners saying WELCOME HOME TODD. My friends came running out and threw me an amazing homecoming celebration.

I was home, and what a long journey it had been. But it was far from over.

The hot and humid temperatures of summer lingered into the cooler air of autumn. The new school term began for my friends, but not for me.

I was alone and having to face the fact that my life was dramatically different. The only positive side to this was the cute homebound teacher, Ellen, my parents hired to help me with my school work.

Acclimating to life at home took time because I no longer had the luxuries of the hospital and was still moving incredibly slowly. I couldn't just push a button to get what I wanted. No more bottle next to the bed to relieve myself. I had pain pills, but they weren't nearly as effective as the shot, especially since I'd built a tolerance to the pain medication.

Less than eight weeks had passed since the accident and I was still struggling. I had endured twenty-eight surgeries. A thin film of skin had been peeled off my stomach, which made it very painful to move. They used it to cover the back of my right leg. My left thigh looked like a gigantic zipper with all of the stitches running through it.

I was bored, lonely, and in pain.

My friends were great about dropping by regularly to see me, and I appreciated it, but their visits didn't compensate for all I was missing.

When I went to my first football scrimmage, I leaned on my crutches along the sidelines as I watched the game. I couldn't walk yet and my muscles had atrophied. I was no longer the defensive threat of the previous two years. I smiled and cheered for my friends in an effort to disguise my deep feelings of sadness. I felt weak, crippled, and useless.

I kept lightheartedly telling myself and others, "Next year!" They were polite and encouraging.

I should have been grateful I was even alive. I knew I needed to take it one step at a time – I should patiently wait for my wounds to heal, learn to walk again, and then think about sports. But I wanted to be finished with it now. I didn't want to wait, or go through the painful healing process.

Each step of the way, my perpetual question was directed to God, "Why aren't you answering my prayers?"

I've since realized we may not know where our steps are leading us, but we do know what steps we can take today. No matter what the situation is, we need to constantly make the most of each step, not begrudgingly, but with gratitude, hope, and faith.

God has a plan for each of us, and that plan is unique, wonderful, and full of good. We may not recognize what it is right away, especially when things are tough and discouraging, but this is not the time to quit. It's the time to be strong, and know each challenge will be an opportunity for our greatness to shine through, not only to bless us, but to bless others.

Though I regularly attended church with my family, I never thought much about how God worked in my life. Church was a place to hang out with my friends on the weekend. Sometimes a group of us would find a back room where we would play spin the bottle with the girls. Church summer camps were about meeting new friends, and maybe having a girlfriend for a few days.

Speaking of girls, I wasn't very confident with them before the accident, and now, due to my disfigurement, I wasn't at all. This was extremely challenging because it was the beginning of high school, a time when dating is a big part of the social scene.

"I hate this thing!" The metal brace I wore was an embarrassment. It kept my paralyzed foot from dragging along the ground, but it also rubbed my calf raw. It gave me sores which became infected, and this made it even more difficult and painful to walk.

However, thankfully, as my semester at home progressed, there were some really great times.

"Todd, will you be our football coach?" asked DeAnn.

To help with the lack of being able to spend time with my friends at school, the ninth grade girls asked me to be the head of the girl's Powder Puff football team. These girls knew how to make me feel proud again, and we all laughed a lot.

There wasn't anything puffy about these girls. They were lean and tough and probably hit harder than many boys. It was a great year for us, especially considering we took second place in the Powder Puff league.

I found my studies at home to be easy, and my grades were good, but upon returning to the classroom during the second semester, I realized I was behind. Though my tutor did a great job, I hadn't been able to put the kind of time into my studies necessary to keep up with my peers.

I'd been dealing with the injury, the loss of social interaction, and now I was failing in school. It seemed all of my dreams were being shattered.

CHAPTER FOUR

The Decision

Our marketing director, Liz, peeks her head around my office door.

"Todd, we got a press release on something called the '50 Peaks Project' in the mail today," she says, handing me a FedEx package. I curiously read the letter describing a Chicago-based organization's intentions of taking a group to climb the highest elevations of all fifty states.

"The team will be comprised of five disabled persons: an asthmatic, a blind person, a person with muscular dystrophy, a senior citizen, and a leg amputee. We have filled the first four slots and are looking for a leg amputee to join us. There will also be guides and an appropriate emergency support team. If you know of someone who might be interested, have them apply before August 31st."

Something stirs inside of me as I read the letter and look at the photographs of the majestic mountains. This is a way I could get back into a more active outdoor lifestyle. But climbing mountains? That's a long shot considering how little physical activity I've participated in since the accident. Maybe it's a way for me to do something I once loved, but never had the opportunity to do. This is definitely bigger than anything I have ever dreamed of doing.

People in my office have mixed emotions about it. Some think it would be a great adventure, "That would be incredible! Maybe the company could help sponsor you." Others caution me against the dangers, "I wouldn't risk it. Be realistic! So many things could go wrong."

My adrenaline starts pumping as I think about it, and I realize reality isn't as much of a concern as is this new opportunity to live a dream.

Once at home I attempt to get some sleep, but am overcome with restlessness. The Santa Ana winds are blowing hot off the desert and across my little island which lay next to Newport Beach, California. Throwing back the blankets, I toss and roll, knotting the sheets as new thoughts ricochet throughout my brain.

What would climbing the highest peaks be like? Mount Whitney, Mount Hood, Denali – they're only names. Where are they? What would they be like to climb? From the news footage I've seen of rescues in the past, I know they're dangerous for even experienced two-legged climbers.

Who do I think I am even imagining such a thing? How can a leg amputee challenge those killer mountains? I can't even walk up the steps at the office without being in pain or out of breath. I must be insane to think anyone could succeed at such a feat with only one leg.

Then, my mind turns quietly to that fateful decision qualifying me to consider the challenge.

Whether in Tulsa, Kansas City, or Salt Lake City, the beige walls of the doctors' offices all looked the same. Each also held the same meaning for me – hope and pain followed by disappointment. And here I was again, sitting on the crinkly edge of the examination table in a skimpy gown waiting for the physician to return.

This time I was in Boston, Massachusetts.

The question? Whether or not I should have my leg amputated.

Idly, I rubbed my inflamed leg and gazed at the customary poster on the far wall – the colorful one vividly illustrating the structure of the human leg and foot. Unfortunately, I was missing some of the parts on the chart.

My thought wandered to the endless number of times during the last seven years I sat like this, waiting for the results of further tests, X-rays, or cultures taken on my foot which was riddled with infection. I was forced to leave college because of it, but landed a well-paying job as a petroleum land man.

As I traveled with the petroleum company I attended many churches. For the first time in my life I was really studying the Bible and was appreciating my growing understanding of God.

However my foot continued to hamper my life. Since the accident, I hadn't gone a week without having a sore somewhere on my leg.

My right leg was paralyzed below the knee because the propeller cut out several inches of my sciatic nerve, along with my hamstring. The advantage was I couldn't feel any pain there. The down side of it was it kept getting infections. It always started inside my heel – a blue-black blood clot the size of a silver dollar under my skin. When I walked, the skin would break, leaving round rings of blood behind – on the floor, in the shower, in my bed.

The wound refused to heal, but I refused to slow down. Then, as the infection crawled up my leg, it attacked my lymph nodes. The swelling and pain spread into my thigh and groin. My ankle remained perpetually swollen from the ulcer. Constantly hurting, I found it difficult to maintain a positive attitude about life. It went on for so long I couldn't remember what it was like to be cheerful. It felt like things might never get better.

Sitting there in the doctor's office, waiting again, I remembered the time when I was sixteen and went hunting with my dad. We traipsed through the woods all day. When we got home, I threw off my muddy boots to find my right sock red with blood and muddy with dirt. Upon closer inspection, I discovered a nail protruding through my boot and sock, straight into the flesh of my foot. I'd apparently walked on it all day without feeling a thing.

I was tired of being sick from the infections. I'd spent my teen years in and out of hospitals in an attempt to stop it. Surgeons had snipped muscle tissue and chiseled away at the bone. This was always followed up with heavy doses of IV medication. I knew my foot was literally killing me, an inch at a time.

I looked down at my flaming appendage and sighed, "God, this just can't go on any longer."

The door opened, and Dr. Roger Emerson walked into the examination room. The Harvard-trained physician sat down on his stool and told me the results of the tests, "We can take skin from your shoulder and try to transfer it onto your heel . . ."

I began shaking my head before he finished. "No. No way! I've gone a similar route before and it didn't work. What would happen if we simply treated the infection?"

"It will continue to spread, Todd, into other bones in your body." He frowned and shook his head slowly. "There's no skin on your heel. It's exposed muscle. The bone will continue to chip off causing more infections. You are already enduring excruciating pain in your upper leg and groin. It will only get worse."

I frowned as I thought about his warning. I'd flown all the way to Massachusetts General Hospital in Boston to see Dr. Emerson. He was one of the country's foremost orthopedic surgeons. My Uncle Bill, a retired colonel from the United States Army, had suggested the medical center as a last-ditch effort to save my leg.

"If we amputate the leg, will it take care of the infection?" I asked slowly.

Dr. Emerson examined my foot once more before speaking, "Yes. I think so. The infection is all in the lower part of your leg." He pointed at the inflammation. "That would take care of the infection."

I wanted to be healthy again.

I had searched deeply for spiritual answers about my life since the accident. I spent many hours, many nights, praying for my leg to be healed. I knew God's will was not for me to be unhealthy. I wondered if having my leg amputated, which would finally rid me of all infection, might be the answer. If so, then this would be a sort of victory, and I needed to have faith in God to see me through.

"Fine! Let's do it!" I sounded more confident than I felt.

The doctor cocked his head to one side. "Just like that? Amputate? Are you sure you don't want to think about it first?"

I shook my head emphatically. "That's all I've been thinking about for the last two years."

"It's not a reversible procedure, you know."

"I understand, sir." With such an important decision looming, it was important for me to further confide, "I also know God wants me to be healthy, and I'll never be healthy as long as I keep having these infections."

He looked relieved. For once he didn't have to convince a patient that amputation was the best treatment. This time there wouldn't be a long wait during which the patient deteriorated, finally becoming too weak for surgery to be an option.

"All right, then. We'll schedule the operation for tomorrow if we can find you a room." He scribbled something on my chart, then looked up. "Why don't you get dressed while I have my nurse make a few phone calls."

I dressed with eager anticipation. Finally, something was going to be done. No more infections and no more fevers. I knew my strength would return. I hurried out to the waiting room to tell my uncle and my dad.

"Are you sure you want to do this?" my father asked.

"Absolutely."

Before long, Dr. Emerson appeared. He looked grave.

"Oh no," I groaned. "Don't tell me I'm going to have to wait."

"Not necessarily," the physician paused, then continued, "I found you a room, but I'd like you to see it before we actually check you into the hospital. It's in the old wing."

"Great!"

"Well, let's go take a look before you get your hopes built up too high," he cautioned. "Remember Mass General is an old hospital – it's been around for a very long time. And the available room is located in the oldest part of the complex."

The doctor led the way. While we walked he explained the surgery procedure and the recovery period. We proceeded down the labyrinth of narrow hallways, dodging ventilators, gurneys, and miscellaneous equipment. Nurses and other medical personnel rushed by in a hurry to wherever they were going.

Dr. Emerson paused to check the number over the doorway with the one on his clipboard. He gave me an, "I warned you" look, then pushed open the door. He gestured for me to enter the room which would be my home for several weeks following the amputation.

Multiple coats of white paint covered the walls of the tiny cubicle. The window looked out onto red brick walls and a wrought-iron fire escape. Faded bedspreads covered the two metal army cot-like beds which were crammed close together military style. I gazed about the drab little room and sighed, wondering how I could cope with the emotional experience of having my leg amputated in such a dreary place.

"Is this it, Doctor?"

"I'm afraid so, Mr. Huston, at the present." He exhaled. "However, if you are willing to wait a month, I can get you into the Phillips House."

I shot him a quick look. "What's the Phillips House?"

He chuckled. "The Phillips House speaks for itself." He led us from the room and back down the hallway as he explained, "It's all part of the same hospital, but it's where wealthy people from all over the world come for their medical needs."

After a long walk through a maze of halls, he led us into what seemed like an exquisite old mansion instead of a hospital. All was quiet. Instead of the bustle of people and equipment cluttering the halls, a calm pervaded the area. Our shoes clicked on the gray marble floors. Dr. Emerson smiled as I entered a large room with its plush, upholstered easy chairs and an expensively draped oversized bed. Wallpaper covered the walls. Opposite the foot of the bed was a large brick fireplace with a Persian area rug in front of the hearth.

I strode over to the window, pulled back the flowered drapery, and glanced out at what seemed to be a park.

Doctor Emerson stepped up behind me. "That's the Charles River. See those boats? Harvard rowing teams. Follow it out and you'll see MIT, Harvard, and Cambridge."

Turning slowly, I let the drapery drop back into place. "I think I want to wait for the surgery, sir."

"Are you sure you want to wait thirty days?"

My uncle, a former army colonel, spoke in a low voice to my father. "Tell him to stay in the other room."

"No." I shook my head emphatically. "I've been in and out of hospitals for seven years. I know how important my attitude will be to my healing. I'll do better if I wait."

The doctor agreed. Later that day my dad and I flew home to wait the required length of time. Over and over, during those thirty days, I questioned the wisdom of having my leg removed. I reminded myself there'd be no going back, no way to reattach it if I changed my mind.

One of the ideas continually recurring was the thought that maybe, just maybe, God would heal me miraculously. I prayed I'd awaken one morning with a brand new healthy foot, or medical research would come up with an alternate solution.

"Dear God," I prayed, "if you save my leg, I promise I'll never do anything bad again. I promise I'll become a preacher." I made many promises.

As the month drew to a close, I realized I needed to make my decision based on the facts, not on the possibility of a miracle or wish. I knew things couldn't go on as they were. If I must sacrifice one portion of my body in order that the rest could live, I would do so. I chose a life and a lifestyle over a leg.

When it was time for me to return to Boston I insisted that my parents stay in Tulsa.

"I can manage this alone," I assured them. "I know I'm doing the right thing."

Reluctantly they agreed to stay.

As I kissed my mother good-bye and gave my dad a hug at the Tulsa airport, they lovingly told me their prayers would go with me.

All I could think of as the jet taxied out onto the runway was, "Finally I'm going to get rid of the pain and infections. Finally I'll feel normal again." I'd forgotten what it was like to live anything resembling a normal life.

The night before the surgery I checked into the hospital and was taken to the Phillips House as arranged. I was prepared for a rugged night of tossing and second-guessing myself regarding whether or not I'd made the right decision.

After the last medical attendant left me for the night, I got out of bed and walked to the window. Pulling back the drapery, I gazed out at the quiet spring night. Shards of light from a crescent moon glistened on the quiet surface of the Charles River. Beyond the park, lights from the surrounding apartment buildings spilled out onto rain puddles dotting the city sidewalks. Silhouettes of elm and maple trees touched the indigo sky. I could also see the lights of Cambridge, Harvard, and MIT. It brought mixed emotions, at times nervous, at times calm.

"OK, God, you saved my life for a purpose. Will you help me now? Where are you in all of this? I'm ready for you to heal my leg now." I'd harbored that hope since I was fourteen.

As I waited, not knowing what to expect, His power did come to me. But not through the touch of a divine hand reconstructing my leg.

He came to me in a whisper.

A gentle rush of God's power filled me with the peace and knowledge that He would see me through the storm I faced in the morning. I felt His presence and His love.

Though the outside remained the same, inside, I changed. I began to see I didn't need to look to the outside world for my peace and joy; if that's where I expected it to come from, life would be a roller coaster ride filled with highs and lows. I could sense the rising conviction that within me was everything I needed to be able to live the peaceful life I craved. Maybe I wasn't going to be healed like I wanted. But my faith did give me a relationship with Him which would see me through all of life's coming challenges.

Like a trusting five-year-old, I slid beneath the cool crisp sheets and fell instantly asleep.

The doctor scheduled my surgery at the last of the day so any infectious tissue he removed would not accidentally contaminate other patients. The aroma of anesthetics lingered in the air as they wheeled me into the operating room.

I wanted to put my newfound inner strength to the test, so I arranged to be awake during the surgery, with only a local anesthetic to deaden the pain. Furthermore, I'd had so many operations over the years that I hated the groggy feeling and nausea following a general anesthetic.

By the way they looked at me, I knew the medical team thought I was strange to have made such a request.

"You know," I joked as the nurses hooked me up to the appropriate machines, "you should come down to my room after we get done here. I plan to order a giant pizza. They do deliver here in Boston, don't they?"

When the anesthetist rolled me onto my side and stuck the needle into my spine, I winced. The spinal block, while initially painful, would deaden the lower half of my body, I took a deep breath. Any second thoughts were gone now. Slowly a tingling numbness traveled from my waist to my feet. I glanced up at the IV bottle beside me, then followed its drips to the tube leading to the needle in my vein.

One of the nurses checked the flow from the IV. "You must be crazy to do this awake."

I understood why she felt this way, so explained, "No, not really. I actually feel very sane. The way I've come to see it is that being able to walk into adversity, and know you can lean on God for comfort and inner strength, well, it's the sanest way to go about life."

I watched Dr. Emerson draw a map on my leg to indicate where the incision would be made. I glanced up at the person on my right side. Instead of a member of the surgical team, I felt the presence of an angel standing beside me, shining down at me.

They covered my face so I couldn't see the actual procedure, and so I would not breathe any of the germs from the rotting tissue.

"This is it," I thought, "No going back now!" I felt gentle tugs as the doctor pulled on my leg muscles and cut through the tendons.

Suddenly, the whir of the saw filled the room.

"This is insane!" The anesthetist stared down at my face. "Are you in pain?"

"No, I'm fine," I assured him. "God is taking care of everything."

I glanced over at my heartbeat registering on the monitor. My heart raced, then settled down again. Feeling a little lightheaded, I closed my eyes to block out the glare from the light above the table.

Once they were done, the doctors sewed me up and the attendants prepared to return me to my room. Curious, I lifted my leg a little. It felt lighter than usual, and shorter. When it dropped, it fell like a cannon onto the gurney. I glanced over at one of the attendants in surprise.

He grinned. "That's the IPOP."

I nodded. Before the surgery the doctor explained they would wrap the stump of my leg in an IPOP, an Immediate Post-Operative Prosthesis, which would allow me to begin taking steps the very next day. The huge cast with the metal plate and the mannequin like foot was designed to give an amputee a physical and a psychological advantage.

I relaxed and watched the ceiling lights flash by while they wheeled me down the long, brightly lit corridor. As one of the attendants reached to open the door to my room, it flew open.

"Surprise!" My mother burst from the room, followed by my father. In his hands was a giant pizza.

"Mom! Dad! What are you doing here? I thought we agreed you wouldn't make the trip."

My dad grinned. "You agreed. We didn't."

Mom kissed my cheek. "You didn't really think we would let you go through this all alone, do you?"

I smiled through a blur of tears. "Thanks," I whispered.

The next morning, before anyone instructed me to do otherwise, I decided to get out of bed and try to take a few steps. I wanted to be certain I could walk again. I needed the security.

I sat up and swung my feet off the bed and onto the floor. I felt a little weak and dizzy. Slowly, grabbing hold of the bed with my free hand, I stood up and shuffled my feet forward two steps.

"Aaugh!" I gasped from the pain shooting up through my leg, torso, and all the way to the top of my head. All the pain I'd been through since the accident didn't equal the excruciating pain I felt taking those two steps. I dropped back onto the bed seriously second-guessing this decision.

"Oh, God!" I thought, "Will I ever walk again?"

CHAPTER FIVE

Pain and Possibilities

The "50 Peaks Project" aims to help handicapped individuals climb to the highest points in each of the fifty states. Looking into it further, I discover there is a "Highpointers Club" comprised of people who are working on this list of climbs, but only thirty-two people have accomplished it. Needless to say, all of them have been able-bodied, two-legged individuals.

Summiting Mount Everest is considered by many to be the toughest mountain climbing feat in the world, and more than one thousand people have conquered it.

I let out a long, slow whistle.

"Only thirty-two people have achieved what I am about to attempt," I repeat to myself, feeling the weight of my words.

What am I thinking? Me, climb mountains? It wasn't so long ago I was lying in a hospital bed feeling like I might never walk again.

My body in agony, I pressed the Call button. "Hurry! Please hurry! I've got to have something for this pain!" Flames shot up my thigh, into my groin, and everywhere else.

The door opened. A nurse popped into the room. "May I help you, Mr. Huston?"

"I'm in a lot of pain," I gasped, wiping a layer of sweat from my brow. "I tried to walk and . . ."

She looked at me with disdain. "You should have waited for us to help you." She hurried to my bedside and helped me back under the sheet. "Stay there and I'll go see what the doctor has ordered for you."

I sighed and laid back against the pillow, shielding my eyes with my free arm. "Please hurry."

Demerol, Percocet, Morphine, Percodan, Tylenol with codeine; the brand mattered little, as long as it soothed my pain. It seemed I had little choice; my only options were to take the mind numbing drugs or be in agony.

I had known about people who'd gotten hooked on prescription drugs, and occasionally I wondered if such a thing could ever happen to me. I didn't want to explore the possibility too deeply because I couldn't imagine not being able to numb my pain with the sweet relief brought by the drugs. Furthermore, any concern about the possibility of being hooked vanished when a nurse handed me a small paper cup containing two little capsules. Or better yet, when I received the stick of a needle followed by the euphoric escape from the pain and boredom.

Before leaving the hospital I arranged to undergo a second operation to reconstruct my lip, for cosmetic purposes, and to repair the roof of my mouth. I was born with a cleft pallet, and though my parents had it fixed when I was a baby, it left a scar I was insecure about. Furthermore, I knew repairing the roof of my mouth would clear up a disorder in the tonal quality of my speech.

"Someday I'll be talking in front of large groups of people, and I want them to understand me," I explained to the doctor. I never dreamed how true that would be.

When I was released from the hospital, Bruce, my college roommate from the University of Oklahoma, invited me and my younger brother Scott to stay with him at his parents' home in Boston until I completed the necessary outpatient visits. Scott drove my car to Boston so the two of us could drive back to Tulsa once I was cleared to travel.

I grew stronger and restless. During my weeks of recuperation, Bruce told us about the fun one could have living in Boston.

One Saturday night the three of us attended a party at his friend's house. I wasn't sure how women would respond to my having only one leg. I was extremely self-conscious, however it didn't seem to bother them.

When we left the party, we climbed into my Mazda RX-7, rolled down the windows, and cranked up the stereo. Bruce and I were in the front, while my brother was scrunched up in the back.

We were stopped at a red light when a rusted brown Pontiac Bonneville filled with college-aged guys pulled up next to us.

"Is that your daddy's car?" the guy in the passenger seat yelled.

Bruce replied, "Is that your mama's car?"

"How'd you like me to put a dent in that pretty car of yours?" The driver of the other car revved his engine threateningly.

Bruce glared back. "How'd you like me to put a dent in your face?"

I stared at Bruce in horror. "What are you doing? There are five guys in that car!"

Bruce ignored me. He eased the RX-7 into an empty parking lot. The other car followed, blocking our exit. The doors on both cars flew open. Eight men hopped out – five from their car and three from ours. Of course, I was a little slower than the rest.

I was barely out of the car when four of their five guys lined up in front of us. Scott flexed his fists, trying to look tough. Standing with my crutches, I gripped the hand holds so tightly I was sure I'd leave an imprint in the metal, but I wanted to make sure they wouldn't fly out of my hands if I needed to use them.

Their fifth man circled around behind us as their driver headed straight for Bruce. "I'll take this guy!" he announced, his body coiled and ready to spring.

The situation wasn't looking too promising. I shot a glance toward Bruce in time to see him deliver a solid right-cross in the nose to the driver. Blood spurted in all directions. The man's cry of agony spurred the other men into action. Two lunged at Scott and the other two headed menacingly toward me. I lifted my crutches and started swinging them around, trying to look dangerous. However, I knew I must have looked pretty pathetic hopping around on my one good leg.

Inches before reaching me one of the two men stopped abruptly. "I don't want any part of this!" He batted the air in disgust and turned away.

"Me neither." They all followed suit except for the one who'd pinned Scott. I hobbled over to the two of them as they wrestled on the ground and pulled the attacker off my brother.

Before any of them changed their mind and decided to continue fighting, I raised my hand and slammed my fist into the hood of their car, leaving an indention in the center.

"Now, get out of here and leave us alone!" I shouted, flailing my crutches in the air like a crazy man. They didn't wait for a second invitation. The last guy jumped in and their Pontiac screeched out of the parking lot.

Since the three of us weren't injured, we climbed back into the RX-7 and headed for home.

"That was dumb!" I growled at Bruce.

"Hey, they had it coming," he answered.

"You could have broken the guy's nose," I retorted.

"Good! He had that coming too," he replied indignantly.

Ten minutes later a police car motioned us to the side of the road. After going through the routine questions, one of the policemen asked, "Do you guys know karate or something?"

"No sir," Bruce answered. Scott and I innocently shook our heads.

"Well, we had to take one of the guys back there to the hospital for stitches. You popped him a good one. You broke his nose."

"We were just protecting ourselves."

The policeman shined his flashlight in the front seat and spotted my leg. He admonished us to be on our way. "And no more fighting!"

Bruce rolled up the window as the patrolman strode back to his vehicle.

"How could you say we don't know karate?" Scott asked.

Bruce replied, "Like it would've been a good idea to tell the guy we've all taken it. Prime lawsuit material there!"

"Hey," I reminded them, "they'd have been laughed out of court once the jury realized there were five of them and three of us, and then saw my stump!"

"So, what's next on the agenda?" Bruce's eyes danced wickedly.

I glanced at my watch, "I think it's time we headed back to your house. Your parents will be worried."

"Yeah, you're right," Bruce admitted, and then grinned. "Let's go home and have a bowl of Friendly's ice cream. It's the best tasting, you know!"

I smiled to myself. Good old Bruce. A great friend, if I could survive him.

The month of recuperation passed and Dr. Emerson released me from his care. Scott and I said our good-byes to Bruce and his family, thanked them for being wonderful hosts, and started for home. The hot, humid summer weather stayed with us as we toured New York City and Washington D.C.

As the RX-7 sped along the interstate across the central states, I glanced over at my brother driving my car. "I hope you know how much I appreciate you, Scott. If I was alone and something happened I'd be pretty helpless."

He smiled in return.

On the way through Kentucky, we stopped to see my girlfriend, Claire, the cutest little southern girl in the world. She was five foot two with chestnut brown hair and eyes. The only drawback was she lived six hundred miles away.

Before we arrived at the house, I fretted about her reaction to me after the amputation. I shouldn't have. She greeted us warmly.

"I was in tears the whole day you were having surgery," she said. I was so busy thinking about her reaction to the amputation I'd been clueless to her thoughts and feelings.

In spite of the medication I was on while we visited, I remembered every detail of the few hours we spent together.

Upon arriving back in Tulsa, I enrolled in classes at the University of Tulsa. I hoped I could convince Claire to go there with me, but due to finances, she chose not to. We continued writing to one another.

I discarded the IPOP and the doctors fitted me for my first custom-fitted artificial leg. I had high hopes for this leg. I was envisioning something comfortable and attractive.

Was I ever disappointed.

The leg was heavy, made of hard fiberglass and wood, with a rigid and cumbersome rubber foot bolted to it. I had to wear an elastic belt around my waist to help hold it in place, which gave me a geriatric appearance. This did not help my physical or emotional recovery – or my prospects with the girls.

For an active guy of twenty-one, the prosthesis was torture to wear. It made me self-conscious. Not only did I detest the way it looked through my clothing, I hated the way it prevented me from doing all the things I loved most. Uncomfortable and bulky, I couldn't take more than four or five steps without feeling pain. Like before the amputation, I was again dealing with swelling, sores, and blisters. When I removed it, my prosthetic sock would be blood soaked. Then I was forced to go without the leg to let it heal.

Life became unpredictable because I never knew when my leg would be well enough to wear my prosthesis. It made it difficult to concentrate on my class work and I couldn't make any plans. I thought the amputation would free me from all of this and I would be able to live my life as I'd always imagined. Except for the lack of any further infection, not much had changed for the better. It was a bitter pill to swallow considering everything I'd been through, and I began to wonder if the amputation was all for nothing.

In order to keep active I went to the gym and worked out my upper body, but the pain and discomfort in my leg kept me from doing cardiovascular workouts.

Continued pain meant continued pain medication, and I began to feel like I couldn't live without it.

Being hooked on the medication made my rehabilitation more difficult. I grew easily agitated and lethargic. I found myself taking drugs rather than doing the things I should be doing. Not only was I wasting my life away, I was also destroying the relationships that were important to me. Worse yet, I knew living from one "fix" to the next wasn't God's purpose for me.

The use of prescription drugs intensified. I enjoyed the euphoria they afforded as well as the relief from pain. I found myself exaggerating the pain as an excuse to ask for more pain medications.

Mornings were when the lethargy hit the hardest. I lost every bit of enthusiasm to attend classes.

Sometimes I would take the pills every other day to increase their effectiveness. When I did this, I experienced withdrawal symptoms, becoming nervous and shaky. Then I interpreted this normal discomfort as a pain needing medication.

My parents watched and worried over my drug use.

"Todd," my father would say, "aren't you taking more medication than you really need?"

"No! You can't know the pain I feel or the amount of drugs I need to take." I tightened my jaw in defiance, determined to justify my behavior. "Don't try to tell me if I feel pain or not. You don't know what it's like to have a leg amputated."

I convinced myself I was handling the medication well. I would hold off taking it until after the day's classes, and I was careful to never drive under the prescription's influence. But my tolerance level for it increased, forcing me to alternate between the different prescriptions.

My eating habits became more erratic. I would go without eating for days so I had an empty stomach when I took the medication. This intensified my highs. Occasionally, I admitted I had a problem and I would try to stop, but inevitably I returned to the drugs within a few days, using them more heavily than before.

Night after night, when I could sleep, I dreamed of a Kansas wheat field, with a blue sky and gentle rolling grasslands. I ran along a well-worn path cutting through the field, totally free of my artificial leg – no pain, no awkwardness, just totally free.

But the dream was over with the dawn, and the reality hit. I wasn't free. I would never be free.

Claire and I continued writing to one another and visited when we could. With the distance, it was easy to hide my drug problem from her and she never knew about it.

We became engaged, but within a short time we both realized the distance between Kentucky and Oklahoma made our courtship almost impossible to maintain. Without anger, but not without pain, we broke our engagement.

One summer day in 1984 I took four tablets of Demerol. Within fifteen minutes, my forehead and face felt numb. A buzzing sound commenced inside my head. My sight blurred. I could tell I was slipping in and out of consciousness. I stumbled down the stairs to the living room where my father was reading the paper.

"Dad." My tongue felt dry and cottony. "I think I overdosed on my pain medication."

My father looked at me with concern. "Let's call the pharmacist to see what to do."

He hovered over me while I placed the call. "Should I come in and have my stomach pumped?" I was scared.

"No, you probably are not in any danger from taking only four tablets. However, everyone is different, so I say that with caution." He warned me about abusing my medication.

I sat on the edge of the couch with my hands clasped together. It was time I took responsibility for my addiction, however I couldn't get over this problem alone. I knew the only way for my imprisonment to end would be to humbly turn to God and reach out for the power which carried me through my amputation. I'd tried to use my human will to get over the pain killers numerous time, but it was to no avail.

I reached out to God with my whole heart and mind. "God, get me out of this and I'll never do it again," I said with stern resolution. And I meant it.

Instantly, my mind cleared. The buzzing in my head stopped. All signs of drowsiness and lingering euphoria disappeared. I got up off the bed, collected the hidden half-empty bottles of medication, and placed them in the medicine chest in the bathroom.

I learned something very valuable that day. I learned once a person makes the decision they want to change something in their life, and especially if they want to change something for the better, they are only one decision away from making that change. And one decision only takes a moment to make. If they put their passion behind that decision and live it, moment by moment, before they know it the years and decades will slip by and they will no longer be imprisoned by whatever was holding them back.

Interestingly, I didn't suffer the typical withdrawal symptoms, nor did I desire the pain killers again.

A month later I swore off all other drugs, including aspirin, alcohol, and caffeine. Except for occasions like a sprained ankle or wisdom tooth removal, I never returned to them.

Again, I saw that God made us as much greater than mere physical beings who are trying to muddle our way through life. He made us as strength, love, wisdom, and many other wonderful qualities. When we begin to live from this standpoint, we experience His power in ways we could never imagine.

Not long after that I heard about an amputee's ski clinic in Tahoe, California. My family encouraged me to attend. I resisted at first because I didn't want to hang around with disabled people. I wanted to be seen as normal. The idea of spending a week with fellow amputees, all discussing their aches and pains like little old ladies in a sewing circle, sounded boring. With a great deal of reluctance I finally agreed.

Was I in for a surprise!

Nearly one hundred people of all ages attended. I was assigned a roommate named Steve, who'd lost his arm in a washing machine accident. We had the greatest time learning to ski. I made many great friends.

By the end of the week my attitude about disabled people changed. I discovered them to be like everyone else. While they had disadvantages due to their injuries, these people loved life. I was chosen, along with a pretty blue-eyed girl named Lori, to be photographed on the chairlift for some promotional material.

I went home from California with a new attitude. The wooden prosthesis continued to bother me, causing me pain every couple of steps, however I went on with life.

One thing I did was enroll in classes at the University of Tulsa and finish my undergraduate degree in finance. After graduation, I crisscrossed the country, picking up jobs here and there in California, Texas, and Tennessee. Still restless, I headed to California for graduate school. I decided I wanted to be a psychologist.

There I met and fell in love with Jessie, a captivating young woman from New Zealand. She was perky, witty, and had a great accent.

After only three months of dating, the subject of marriage popped up. A brisk December wind whipped about us as we sat on a rock at the beach watching the surf break on the shore.

"Todd, I heard from immigration today about my Visa." Jessie drew imaginary circles on my pant leg.

"Oh?"

"It's about to expire. They're going to send me back to New Zealand."

"No!" I protectively drew her into my arms. I loved Jessie. The thought of her being an ocean away terrified me. I didn't want to lose her because of distance, as I had lost Claire. "There must be something we can do."

"If we got engaged . . ."

My heart leaped at the idea. Marriage! That's the answer!

The week before Christmas we flew to Tulsa and got married in my parents' home.

From then on I worked harder than ever at my studies, as well as holding down a job in the psychiatric ward in a local hospital. During exams I would go as long as thirty-six hours without sleep.

Second semester came and went with the usual work, classes, friends, and fun.

We were only married a short time when Jessie began chiding me about my missing leg. Day by day, she chipped away at my self-esteem, complaining I kept her from being as free and active as she wanted to be.

41

It was like a knife cutting away pieces of my heart every time she complained.

When we first met we attended church together. This had been important to me during our courtship. I believed we shared the same goals and spiritual beliefs. But soon it became apparent we were poles apart.

A year into the marriage, we hit a major snag. Jessie admitted to having had an affair with the husband of a couple we knew.

"Why, Jessie?"

"Well. . ." She hesitated before driving the knife into my heart again. "I guess I liked the freedom I had with him. It sounds silly, but he could run and carry me in his arms, things you will never be able to do."

Somehow we picked up the pieces of our relationship and promised one another to work at making our marriage a success.

Even though it was difficult to focus on my studies because of the marriage problems, I struggled to the finish. I graduated with my master's degree in psychology and found employment as a psychiatric assistant in the children's psych ward at a local hospital. While the job didn't pay much, I enjoyed working with the children, helping them face problems in their lives.

Jessie belittled my new position and the amount of money it generated. Living in Southern California was expensive. Each month it took our combined checks to survive. As her two-year temporary immigration status passed she became more and more restless.

"If you would quit your job and look for work up near Hollywood I know I could find work in the movie industry. You know that's always been my dream. It's why I came to the U.S. in the first place." Her petulant little mouth quivered and her clear green eyes filled with tears.

I reached out to her to gather her in my arms. She resisted. I sighed. I wanted to be supportive. I had tried to catch a glimpse of her dream since the first time she voiced it. But I loved my job and living on Balboa Island.

But more than any of that, I dreaded the possibility of losing the one with whom I'd chosen to spend the rest of my life.

However, I soon found out you can try everything to make someone happy, only to find everything isn't enough.

CHAPTER SIX

Dreams of Running

I search for a glimpse of Denali as I step out of the bunkhouse, but it's hidden behind a curtain of mist and clouds.

I think back to the day I first heard of the "50 Peaks Project." Up to that point I never imagined I would hike again, much less climb mountains.

Though I trained hard for this expedition, and proved my mountaineering abilities on some extremely difficult mountains in the lower forty-eight, doubt begins to creep in again.

This mountain is different.

I pray my hopes and dreams won't be shattered in disappointment.

The loaded van sped down the Pacific Coast Highway in Los Angeles. "Do it again, Mr. Huston. Do it again!" the children shouted. "Take off your leg again." The driver of the van laughed as they begged me to remove my artificial leg.

We enjoyed a great day at the beach but I hurt most of the day from the small particles of sand that managed to creep in between the prosthesis and my stump. The sand acted like sandpaper on my scars and tender skin, so when we loaded the van for our return to the adolescent psychiatric hospital, I unfastened my artificial limb. The kids shrieked with delight when I allowed them to take my leg and hang it out the van window for drivers of the passing vehicles to see.

I liked working with children. Many of the rewards were instantaneous. Jessie didn't like it. She wanted to leave the hospital's employ and move closer to Hollywood.

"But I'm doing what I feel God wants me to do," I answered.

"God?" she fired back. "He doesn't care about us!"

I was shocked. "How can you say that?"

Her vehemence disarmed me. I thought I married a woman who was spiritual, who believed in God like I did.

After the continued pressures, I relented. I agreed to quit my job and move to Hollywood. I gave a two-week notice at our apartment.

One evening, as I prepared to attend a midweek meeting at the church, I asked Jessie to go with me. She hadn't attended church for some time. I noticed she seemed agitated and nervous, but I didn't give it much thought since she was often restless.

"Are you sure you won't go with me?" I asked.

She shook her head. "No, I'd rather not."

"Well, do you want me to stay here with you?"

"Oh, no," she answered hastily. "I'll be fine, really."

"OK." I kissed her on the cheek and left. "We'll spend some time together when I get home, OK?"

"Sure."

I enjoyed the service and headed for home. I thought about Jessie. My mind was in a state of total confusion. It seemed everything I did was wrong in her eyes. I didn't know what I could or couldn't say without making her upset or grow cold and cruel. It seemed this was another chronic problem in my life, and I couldn't figure out what to do to fix it. How was I going to go through a lifetime of this?

When I parked our car in front of our place, I thought it was strange that all the lights in the apartment were out. I climbed the stairs and unlocked the front door.

"Jessie? Jessie?" No answer. I wondered if maybe she was asleep, so I tiptoed into the living room, expecting to hear the television going and to find her curled up on the sofa. But all was silent. I immediately sensed something was wrong. The sound of my footsteps echoed off the walls as I crossed the room and peeked into our bedroom. I flipped on the light and gazed about the room. The sliding closet doors were open and revealed a dark emptiness where her clothing had been. Framed photos, her perfume bottles – missing. Her dresser drawers were on the floor, bare and abandoned. On the desk, I found a note. A lump grew in my throat as I read her message.

"Dearest Todd, I'm sorry, but I'm so confused. I need to get away for a while to do some thinking about us and our relationship. I hope you can find it in your heart to forgive me."

I was dazed, like a train slammed into me and ripped my heart out. The paper flitted to the floor. I wondered what happened and where she was. I couldn't figure out what all of this meant. Exhausted from the anxiety, I collapsed on the couch. I hoped it was just a nightmare, and when I woke up she would be back.

I then noticed the top drawer of the desk was partly opened. My heart and mind raced. I opened it the rest of the way and discovered our checkbook was gone. I rushed through the apartment, searching for traces of Jessie. Only the aroma of her perfume lingered to remind me of her.

I couldn't believe it. She was gone. She'd stayed with me long enough to get her green card, her permanent Visa, which didn't require her to be married.

I buried my head in my hands. "Oh, God! What next? This is more than I can take."

Suddenly I felt claustrophobic. I had to get out. I couldn't stand being alone in our apartment. It held too many painful memories. Everywhere I looked, I saw Jessie. I grabbed my jacket and took off into the night.

I wandered down along the shore. The water gently lapped at the wooden pilings of the docks. The stars stood out in bold relief against the moonlit sky. The bells on the sailboats in the bay tinkled lightly. The light of the city dotted the hillside behind me.

I never felt so alone before in my entire life.

It was as if I was on a deserted island, totally isolated and empty. In my misery I cried, "Oh, God! What am I supposed to do now? She wanted to live near Hollywood, so I gave up everything for her. Now I have no job, no place to live, and hundreds of dollars of bills to pay."

Friends encouraged me to have Jessie arrested and deported for fraud, but I wasn't interested in revenge. I still wanted her back.

I worked up the courage to call her a week later. My heart dropped into my stomach when she answered the phone. The distance in her voice was unmistakable as I tried to reason with her about coming back home.

Hurt, I resorted to the topic I'd sworn to myself I'd never broach with her. "You know, of course, I could go to the authorities and have you deported."

"You try that and I'll lie!" The cold steel in her voice chilled my heart. "If you ever come back at me, I'll tell such big lies about you no one will ever believe you again."

I hung up the receiver, discouraged and heartsick. It baffled me that the woman I loved could become so vicious. I wondered if she ever really loved me. Even though it hurt to think about it, I realized she probably never did.

As difficult as it was, I turned my focus to finding a job. Day after day I looked for work. Night after night I walked down to the dock and stared out over the water, until the pale shades of dawn appeared behind the coastal hills of Newport and Laguna Beach. Then I would walk back to the apartment, shower, and go job hunting again.

One night, after a particularly despairing day, I sat on the pilings at the bay silently listening to the night sounds around me. I was past the point of demanding answers from God. I decided it was time to wait patiently on His direction. When I had decided to marry Jessie, I ran headstrong on my own. This time, whatever I chose to do, I would wait to hear God's will.

Then it came to me – work with amputees.

"Amputees? How can I make money working with amputees? There's no money doing that."

Again, I heard the message, "Work with amputees."

The message was so strong I couldn't deny it. Taking a deep breath, I whispered, "OK, God. If You provide me with the opportunity, I'll do the work."

This decision settled some of the turmoil I was experiencing with decisions regarding employment, but I still felt a great deal of emotional pain with the failure of my marriage. I turned to God for help with that, too.

"If Jessie is gone for good, please help me to forgive her."

At that moment a refreshing peace swept over me, and I felt a sense of calm for the first time in a long time. I leaned back and gazed at the stars, clouds, and moon – an artist's canvas in constant motion. It was as if the heavens had opened up and I knew without a doubt I could trust God's love to create good in my life, both with my job situation and with my need to forgive.

A few weeks later I found full-time employment with NovaCare, the largest artificial limb company in the world. I started as the clinical director of their Amputee Resource Center, visiting recent amputees in the hospital and teaching health-care professionals about the psychology of amputation. I traveled to Washington, D.C. for the Amputee Coalition of America to negotiate with senators and congressmen about improving the health care of amputees.

My co-workers became like family, and helped with the void I'd experienced since Jessie left.

One day a glossy red and gold folder about the *50 Peaks Project* arrived. As I read through the information, something stirred inside of me. This could be a way I could get back into a more active outdoor life. But climbing mountains? I wasn't too sure.

I showed the letter to a couple of friends in the office. Some thought it would be a great adventure, while others cautioned me against the dangers.

Through doing research, I realized only thirty-one people, none of whom were disabled, had successfully climbed all fifty high points. I knew I wanted to go, but I was scared.

If I was being honest with myself, what I was most fearful of was failure. I had experienced enough failure in my life – my leg, my marriage – and I wasn't sure I could handle another defeat.

The back-and-forth argument ensuing within me reminded me of the good and bad angels sitting on either shoulder, duking it out, "Haven't I learned that, with God, I can overcome any challenge? Still, where would I even start? What would I need for supplies? What kind of workout program would I need to get into shape for such a climb? Is this God's plan for me? Just because I'm excited about something does not mean it's God's will."

Throughout that long, restless night, questions raced through my mind. Was this the opportunity I prayed about on the dock the night Jessie left me?

A person I knew I could trust with expert advice was my friend, Fred Zalokar. Fred and his wife Kathy lived in Reno, Nevada, and were good friends of mine from Oklahoma.

I read the letter to him over the phone. "I'd like to do it, but I'm not sure I'd be able to."

"I think you should go for it, Todd," he encouraged. His confidence meant a lot since I knew he would never urge me to do something he didn't think I was capable of doing. But then again, a couple of years ago Fred made me walk the hills of San Francisco on crutches to push start his car.

"I don't even know if I'd get chosen to go, but if I did, would you help me out?"

He answered immediately, "Of course! Kathy and I would do everything we could to help you. You know that."

On my way to work the next morning, I resolved to fill out the application, which I did while on my lunch break. I had a feeling my life was about to change dramatically as I watched the white envelope disappear down the mail chute.

I spent the rest of the day trying to push thoughts of the expedition from my mind and concentrate on performing my daily routines, but I didn't do a very good job at it. The expedition was all I could think about.

I realized embarking on something like this would mean I'd have to get my body into the kind of shape it hadn't been in since the accident seventeen years ago. My survival would depend on just how well I trained. It would be like preparing for battle, a battle against my body as well as my mind.

My thoughts wandered in and out of possibilities. Maybe I wouldn't be chosen to go. Maybe I'd missed the application deadline. Maybe climbing mountains wasn't what God had in store for me.

A week later a packet arrived in the mail from the *50 Peaks Project*. I stared at the return address, frozen with anticipation.

"That doesn't look like a rejection letter," said Pat, one of my co-workers, as she examined the package. "It's too thick."

I said a quick prayer and ripped open the envelope.

A letter dropped out.

I bent down and picked it up, took a deep breath, and began to read.

Dear Mr. Huston:
We are glad to inform you that you have been selected to join the "50 Peaks Project" expedition.

The letter went on to spell out the financial and legal obligations, as well as other bits of information I would need.

"I'm going!" I shouted, giving Pat a high five. "I'm going on the expedition!"

I read through the letter again, letting the words sink into my brain. This was for real!

I noticed Pat was gleaming with excitement at the prospect of her friend getting to experience something so amazing.

The first people I called were my parents. My mother was worried about my physical safety while my father was concerned about my financial well-being.

He stated firmly, "You just got a new job, son. You can't take time off to climb mountains."

Their anxieties were valid. Since receiving the letter and seriously considering doing the expedition, the logical side of my brain thought of little else.

The rest of the afternoon I found it impossible to concentrate on the work stacked on my desk. There was so much to do to get ready. The game plan I'd developed while waiting for the letter began rolling through my mind.

"I need to get my body ready for this," I thought out loud. "I've got to build my endurance and my upper body strength."

"You know," Pat volunteered, "the club I belong to has a rotating rock wall which works something like a treadmill. I bet it would be great for you to train on."

"Great! Sign me up." I needed all the help I could get.

I put a call through to the director of the *50 Peaks Project*. I had a thousand questions to ask. He answered mine, and asked me a couple of his own. "Do you know any serious mountain climbers who might consider being one of our guides?"

Immediately I thought of Fred. If he was along I knew we'd be in good hands. When I spoke with him later he agreed to be a part of the team.

The part of the training I dreaded the most was the running. There I was, at thirty-one years old, needing to learn to run again. I hadn't run since I was fourteen, but sure dreamed about it. My recurring dream was of running through the fields of Kansas with two good legs, the deep blue sky above, and the wind blowing gently through my hair.

Talking with amputee friends who regularly ran helped me believe my goal was achievable. I was determined that if they could do it, so could I.

The fog rolled in from the Pacific one morning as I gazed down the beach, ready and eager to begin my first run. I took a deep breath and swung my arms from side to side to loosen-up. I felt exuberant and alive. I didn't want to overdo it my first time out, so I decided I would run the circumference of the island once and quit.

I charged down the pathway. I had to move to the side as an older woman named Eleanor jogged by me. We waved at one another.

I ran no more than one hundred feet when I collapsed against a fence. My breath came in short, painful gasps. Sea gulls overhead mocked me with their calls. I couldn't believe it! My legs refused to cooperate with one another. They kept hitting each other, causing me to trip. I was afraid I would face-plant onto the path at any moment.

I stumbled to an empty bench and sat down. My heart was pounding and I couldn't suck the air in fast enough. Was I trying to do the impossible? I felt trapped, wondering if my dream of running and being prepared for *50 Peaks* would ever come true. The athlete who could outrun and outmaneuver his opponents on the playing field in junior high was embarrassingly uncoordinated and winded. I stumbled back to my apartment.

All I wanted to do was crawl back onto my couch and rest. Sitting in front of the TV and eating potato chips sounded much better than going through all of this. However, I knew quitting was not an option.

Later that day I saw Eleanor. She laughed, "That's the way it is for two-legged runners too, you know. When we first start running we also spend a lot of time stumbling over our own feet and getting completely out of breath."

Alone that night, I remembered the trials I'd been through: the accident; the many surgeries; the drug addiction; the long, painful recoveries; and my wife's chidings and our subsequent divorce.

"Those were true mountains, Todd," I told myself. "Preparing for this expedition and learning to run again is child's play in comparison."

Yet, I was taunted by the image of myself tripping over my own feet trying to run. All the demons of insecurity rattling around in my brain mocked my dreams.

I knew I had to run. Running would be overcoming a psychological barrier as well as a physical one. If I were ever to experience my dream of being active, hiking and camping, doing all the things I enjoyed as a kid, and especially if I wanted to participate in the *50 Peaks Project*, I had to begin with running. If I stopped trying now, I would probably remain sedentary for the rest of my life – always dreaming, but never doing. This would only make a difficult existence even more disappointing.

The next morning I strapped on my leg, tightened the shoelaces on my rubber foot, and headed out into the foggy sunrise of the Balboa Island dawn. I was determined.

As the fog lifted, I set out running, stumbling, and walking. There was no way I was going to give up this time. I decided to go the hundred feet again. A few steps in, Eleanor jogged past.

"Keep at it," she called over her shoulder as she disappeared around the next bend.

I persisted. For a week I ran one hundred feet. The next week, though it was a strain, I doubled the distance by running the first one hundred feet and walking the second. Every morning as Eleanor passed me she called out encouraging words.

After a month of running every morning, I completed the circle around the island for the first time – 1.6 miles. Totally winded, my legs like rubber, I limped back to my apartment and called my parents to share the thrill of my accomplishment. They tried, but they couldn't understand why I was so excited. My local friends understood my exhilaration, but even they couldn't fully comprehend what 1.6 miles meant to me.

I continued running every morning, farther and farther. One morning as the sun cleared the tops of the coastal range, I decided it was time to fulfill my dream. I would run the dusty trail across two miles of grassy fields, not in Kansas, but in the back bay between Balboa Island and Newport Beach.

Up and down, across the gentle hills, I ran. That day I outran my heartaches. I outran my pain. I outran my loneliness and my fears. It was as if I'd been released from prison. No walls were too high. No bars too strong to hold me. My conviction was strengthening that, through faith, I could do anything.

In three months' time I extended my run from Balboa Island to Laguna Beach, twelve miles up and down hills, without stopping.

Then I thought of Jessie. Now I could be what she claimed she wanted in a husband. But quick on the heels of that thought was the realization that a leg wouldn't make a difference to her. I was beginning to understand people aren't truly happy until they are happy with themselves, and I knew this held true for Jessie, too. I knew it was time to get my head together and face the fact that my marriage was over.

I began to realize everyone's life can be an example of God's power and grace, no matter what circumstances they have gone through. I decided getting distressed over how others treated me would always be a dead end and keep my focus short-sighted. It was time to start serving God with greater dedication by living the love and greatness he created me to be. It was time take all of the lessons I was learning, and the spiritual insights I was gaining, and share them with others. It was time to make a difference in this world.

Over the next few days, while running in the mornings, during idle moments at work, and while falling asleep at night, I thought about nothing but the climb and how it could be an amazing catalyst for sharing the message of overcoming challenges.

Now that I was getting comfortable with running, my next goal was to go kayaking on the ocean. Since I'd maintained my upper body through the years, the days out on the ocean were refreshing and invigorating and strengthened my cardiovascular system. I enjoyed watching the seals playing alongside my Kayak as I made my way down the coast.

I then added hiking and mountain biking to my list of sports. The trails on the hills around Laguna Beach gave me plenty of exercise in the early mornings and weekends, while enlightening me about the reality of the threat rattlesnakes bring to hikers.

My new agility set me to remembering the good times I'd had camping as a Boy Scout and Eagle Scout. I decided I wanted to start camping again, however I wasn't certain I could lug all the necessary equipment on my back while maneuvering the rough terrain.

My first visit to a camping supply store in seventeen years delivered quite a shock. I couldn't even identify half of the equipment being sold. What was Gore-Tex, Whisper-Lite, Dry Rope, fleece, and VE-25. One thing which hadn't changed was the exorbitant prices. Reluctantly, I signed the VISA slip and left the store with a couple of small items. Camping with such pricey gear would have to wait.

"Maybe in time," I told myself.

At least I still had my kayaking and running.

The biggest obstacle to my potential success with the *50 Peaks Project* was my prosthesis. Not the fact that I had to wear one, but the fact that the one I was wearing was made of wood and plastic, was incredibly heavy and cumbersome, and kept falling apart. I'd had it replaced three times since my amputation twelve years ago, however I was never able to afford a leg making use of new technology. The leg they gave me after my amputation, and each subsequent leg thereafter, used the same technology used to create prosthetics since the Vietnam War. Since I'd started putting so much pressure on it during my training, it was continually breaking. Layers of duct tape was all that was holding it together, and I wasn't sure how much longer it would last. I needed something lighter and sturdier. Being able to afford it was a different matter altogether.

Reading my employee benefits package, I discovered the company's insurance benefits would pay up to $1,000 for an artificial limb, so I began shopping around for one. The best deal I could find would cost me $1,500 above the insurance company's portion. I didn't have that much. In fact, I didn't have any money since Jessie had virtually emptied our savings account. I couldn't afford to buy the leg, nor could I afford to go without it.

I decided to let go of my frustration and trust in my faith once again.

Not long after I began shopping for my new leg, my employer switched insurance companies. I hoped this company would offer better benefits, but they didn't.

The continuous cycle of getting my hopes up, only to have them dashed once again, seemed to be never-ending. However I understood the importance of keeping my faith, so I didn't let it wane.

One evening a friend of mine called and talked me into attending a business convention with him in Irvine, California. It was composed of executives who wanted to discuss ideas about how to improve their personal and professional lives.

During the course of the meetings, the fifty people attending were divided into groups of five. Our group found a quiet spot and formed a circle.

Our group leader stated the purpose. "We're supposed to take turns answering two questions: How do I want to be seen by other people, and for what do I want to be remembered."

One by one the members of our group introduced themselves and answered the questions.

"I'd like to be remembered for helping abused children."

"I'd like to be remembered for fostering world peace."

"I want people to remember me for my community service."

Incredibly, three of the members of our group worked for PacifiCare, the insurance company providing coverage for my employer. In fact the president of PacifiCare, Jeff Folick, was part of my group, and was the person who wanted to be remembered for fostering world peace.

When my turn came, I began, "You all are sitting here talking about how you'd like to change the world by doing things like fostering world peace, and these are admirable goals. However, how do we expect to do this when we aren't helping the people right here, in our own back yards, who are positioned to make this global difference?"

I went on to tell them about my life story, and how I had the opportunity to share a message with the world that could truly be a force for good. I told them PacifiCare's policies were hindering me from achieving this goal because they couldn't cover the relatively small amount I needed to purchase the necessary leg. I showed them my duct taped leg and told them about my multiple efforts to purchase the leg doctors recommended, and the walls I continually came up against due to cost restraints.

When I finished speaking, the president of the insurance company responded, "I want to talk with you about this."

By 10:30 the next morning I received a call from a top-level manager at PacifiCare. "We want you to be able to get the leg you want. Start immediately with the fittings, and we'll pick up the cost."

I was elated and grateful. I could see God's hand in bringing Jeff and me together.

CHAPTER SEVEN

Fifty Peaks On My Own?

I sit with the other hopeful climbers at the ranger station watching a National Park Service video about Denali. As the film credits roll, I glance through the window at the overcast cloud bank separating us from the famed mountain. I still haven't caught a glimpse of the Great One yet.

A park ranger walks to the front of the room and turns to stare at us. With a solemn face he asks, "Are you sure you want to go onto this mountain? We've already had climbers die up there this season. One bad step, and it's over."

He pauses to let his words sink in. "You could break through a crevasse and slide down the side of the mountain beneath the surface of the ice. You could disappear through one of them ten feet from your tent. And then there's always the potential for an avalanche."

Fragments of information race through my mind. An avalanche can uproot whole forests, tumbling pine and fir trees as if they are matchsticks, and spewing tons of snow, rock, dirt, and trees into the valleys. Slides have been known to flatten large buildings as if they were Styrofoam cartons. John Muir wrote about an avalanche in the high Sierras that wiped out an entire lake, taking water and fish with it.

The ranger eyes each one of us, carefully studying us as if to determine our competence. "Returning climbers are reporting winds strong enough to brush a man off the side of the mountain. You also need to be prepared for possible whiteout conditions, in which you can become disoriented and freeze to death."

I feel nervous heat rising in my shoulders and my stomach starts to feel queasy. I try calming myself before my breakfast makes a return appearance. Surely all of this is an exaggeration. I had been told rangers will discourage people from going up the mountain. They figure if their tales intimidate someone enough to make them turn back, they don't belong up there. How bad can it really be?

Even as I consider the possibility, I know we aren't listening to fictional accounts. The events he's talking about are true. I begin to wonder why I'm subjecting myself to this. Doubt swirls, spinning uncontrollably in my head. I wonder how I can climb this monster with only one leg when so many two-legged experienced climbers shy away from the challenge. How did I ever get myself into this?

After Jessie walked out on me I joined a singles Bible-study group called *The Becomers*, which met at the Newport Beach St. Andrew's Presbyterian Church. That week I attended the regular Tuesday night meeting. As pumped up as I was about the climb, it took a miracle to help me concentrate on the evening's lesson. Yet I knew I needed the spiritual energy – all of my training was wearing me down.

I told the members of the prayer group about the *50 Peaks Project*. "There will be an asthmatic, a guy with multiple sclerosis, a blind woman, another woman who is seventy years old, and then me, an amputee. I've been training for it, but it would be great to have help, so I wondered if any of you might be interested in hiking with me."

A young blond woman named Lisa volunteered. After the meeting I told her to meet me at my home on Balboa Island and we could hike the cliffs of Corona Del Mar together.

We quickly became friends. Lisa's cheerful nature and upbeat attitude made the climbs fun. In addition to our regular climbs, we talked long hours on the phone, sharing what was going on in our lives.

She knew about Jessie because of the prayer group, and I knew how she'd been a computer graphic artist for Apple Computers. Burned out on corporate life, Lisa recently found work in the Huntington Beach area as a textile designer.

It was great to have someone with whom I could share the excitement of my new job at NovaCare. When I had a presentation to make at a seminar in La Jolla for health-care workers, Lisa attended. Afterward, she gave me some great ideas for strengthening my presentation.

My life seemed to be going in a great direction. However, I was still having trouble letting go of the memory of what Jessie did to me. Though I thought I had forgiven her, I found there was still a strong desire in me to make her pay.

"After all," I kept reasoning with myself, "I have the law on my side."

I knew I could get her expelled from the country, and the officials would never even grant her a visitor's Visa in the future. However, such a prosecution would take an enormous investment of my time, energy, and money. I persistently questioned myself as to whether or not my anger was that strong. Furthermore, I knew if I put so much effort into getting even, I may not have anything left to prepare for the climb.

I realized over the next few months I could choose to put my time, energy, and money into prosecuting Jessie, or I could use it to get ready for a once-in-a-lifetime experience. There was no way I could do both. I had to make a decision. I wanted to go on the climb so badly I could taste it. Yet, letting go and doing nothing to the woman who'd trampled on my trust, self-confidence, and good name – I wasn't sure I could do that.

One evening as I tried to sleep, the war raged inside of me. Frustrated, I made my way down Coral Avenue and sat on the dock, watching the phosphorescent waves dancing in the moonlight and listening to the bells on the sailboats ringing in the wind.

"Which will it be, Todd?" I asked myself. "The mountain, or revenge?"

I knew to truly find peace I needed to give this question to God, and in the stillness of the ocean breezes, I heard the answer. "Let it go."

A part of me wanted to rebel at this answer. I argued, "She shouldn't be able to get away with this!"

Again the message came to me.

"Let it go."

The thought of doing this was incredibly difficult. Though I inherently knew this was best, I felt a deep struggle within.

But I finally did it. I let the anger go and made my decision – the mountains.

Once I turned my feelings of revenge over to God, and focused on preparing for the mountain climb, I had more energy than I believed possible.

For the next few months, after my eight-hour work day, I worked out on the treadmill, StairMaster, and rotating rock wall, followed by body surfing on the ocean later in the evenings. On the weekends I hiked in the mountains around Southern California and rode my mountain bike in the hills outside of Laguna Beach.

There was a fine line between training hard and risking serious injury. I was constantly concerned I could injure myself and not be able to do the climb.

Autumn gave way to winter, and I continued training hard.

I received word the first *50 Peaks Project* meeting would be in Provo, Utah. Since Fred lived in Reno, which was a short drive from Provo, I flew in to meet him and we drove to the meeting together.

The night before the meeting we watched *K2*, a movie about the first two American's to summit the second highest mountain in the world. The dangers, the drama, the near-death experiences, and the helicopter rescue which nearly failed, all left my mouth hanging open throughout the entire movie.

As the credits rolled by, I turned to Fred and declared, "No way! Not me!"

He laughed and told me not to be such a wimp.

At the meeting the organizers supplied us with necessary information and stressed the need for more financial backing for the project. We posed for photos with the other team members, then headed west toward Reno.

"You know, Todd," said Fred, tapping his fingers on the steering wheel, "I've got a bad feeling about this."

"I know what you mean. I wonder if the people organizing *50 Peaks* can actually pull this thing off. They don't have a single sponsor yet."

"It wouldn't hurt to have an alternate plan just in case everything falls through," Fred suggested.

"What do you mean?"

"Would you want to climb the fifty high points on your own?"

I thought about his suggestion for a moment. "I don't know."

"We could help raise money for *50 Peaks*, but begin working on a backup plan, just in case."

I thought about his suggestion. "I wonder if my company would consider sponsoring me." I pondered the possibility during the rest of the ride back to Reno, then again on the flight back to California.

When I talked with the company executives about sponsoring the *50 Peaks Project*, they voted to donate $5,000 to the cause, as well as give me the leave of absence I needed to do the climb.

The holiday season came and went and I had yet to hear from anyone at *50 Peaks*. In January I decided to call them. They had no progress to report. I went out to dinner that night with Lisa and told her some of the *50 Peaks* investors hadn't come through.

"I guess I have some decisions to make. Should I continue with this dream?"

We sat in silence for a few moments.

I continued, "The funny thing is, I really believe God led me into this, and He has big plans for me."

Lisa looked across the table at me and matter-of-factly said, "Then you need to do it. I'll be behind you all the way." She added, "Something you should seriously consider is beginning a journal. If this thing is as big as you believe it will be, you'll want to keep an accurate recording of your day-by-day preparations."

The next day she showed up at my island cottage with a black leather diary.

I talked again with the *50 Peaks* director. Things didn't look much better than they had earlier. I placed the receiver on its cradle and stared idly out the window onto the quiet little street in front of my apartment. The row of weather-beaten houses clung together like a line of fading chorus girls. I rubbed the back of my neck and left shoulder.

Feeling frustrated, I called Whit Rambach, one of the guides for the project. I asked his opinion on the situation.

His thoughts echoed mine – not good. "Todd," he reminded me, "you have enough money to get started on your climb. I'd be happy to forget the *50 Peaks* group and just climb with you. Let me know if that's what you decide."

I walked into the kitchen, grabbed a glass of water, drank it, and paced back into the living room. Deep in thought, I paced back into the kitchen, trying to work through my troubled thoughts.

"Todd, do it on your own." A familiar voice spoke to me.

I stopped. "Do it on my own?"

"Do it on your own." God was giving me permission.

A rush of excitement flooded through me – a feeling of completeness. I darted to the telephone to call Fred. In detail, I told him the latest on the situation with the *50 Peaks Project*. "I don't think they'll be able to do it."

"I've been expecting that," he admitted.

"Let me ask you a question. If I decide to climb the fifty peaks on my own, will you . . ."

With anticipation Fred interrupted me, "Absolutely! Whatever you need! Just let me know how I can help."

I smiled to myself. That's Fred!

Knowing I had his support encouraged me. We talked a few minutes longer about the preparations I needed to make for an independent climb, then signed off.

"By the end of the week I'll have a list of equipment together you'll need."

"Thanks, man."

"Hey, no problem. Let me know if there's anything else I can do to help."

It was happening.

I was going to climb mountains!

CHAPTER EIGHT

Summit America

The look on the ranger's face leaves no doubt in my mind. He knows someone in this room won't make it back.

I hear those familiar thoughts once again. Am I using the climb as a distraction from the pain of the divorce? Am I doing this out of a sense of pride, trying to prove I can do anything a two-legged man can do?

Then I remember God and I have already settled those issues. I'm here to live a message I've been directed to tell.

"Any questions?" The ranger seems to be staring directly at me.

"Yeah," a climber behind me drawls, "when do we leave for base camp?"

A nervous chuckle passes among the first-timers.

The ranger eyes the man, his countenance grim yet professional. "According to the weather service, we need to wait for a break in the clouds on the mountain in order for the air taxi to have a safe takeoff and landing."

"How long can that take?" another hiker asks.

The ranger shakes his head. "Hopefully not long. There are some people we need to get off of it first."

Suddenly, I don't feel as enthusiastic as I did when I initially had the idea to do this climb on my own.

I called Lisa to tell her my decision.

"I think I can do it," I said. "Not only that. I think I can set a new world record, even beating the one set by a non-handicapped person."

"You know I'm behind you." I could hear the smile in her voice.

"I'll need help back here," I confessed. "I was thinking of asking you to operate the business side of the climb."

"Sure," she said enthusiastically. "What do I have to do?"

With my friends so willing to help I knew my chances for success were much greater.

I received mixed reviews when I told people at work about my new plans. Some were excited and wished me the best. Others weren't so enthusiastic and told me I was crazy for even considering it.

Yet inside my heart, I knew this was part of a bigger life-mission being propelled by God.

Whit and I worked out our plans by telephone. He drove down from Fresno to help finalize the logistics of the climb.

To help finance the project I contacted potential sponsors. I received a variety of contributions, ranging from one hundred to five thousand dollars.

The North Face and REI, large suppliers of hiking gear and outdoor wear, agreed to give me a discount on their equipment, along with some freebies.

Roy Snelson, the director of Wings of Calvary, an organization providing artificial limbs for people in Third World countries, also contributed to the climb. In speaking with him about my funding concerns he encouragingly shared, "If God wants you to climb, He will provide."

Hoping for another donation, I explained the change in plans to my employers at NovaCare, but they declined. However, they were designing my leg and weren't charging for the time they were putting into design modifications. This was a huge help because there were numerous modifications necessary to prepare my leg for what I was about to do.

My new leg needed to stand up to the abuse of glacier and boulder hiking, and much of that technology had yet to be created. I was grateful NovaCare's engineers worked with me and were open to my ideas and suggestions.

It's incredibly difficult for amputees to do what I proposed doing during this expedition because a prosthetic leg lacks the abilities of a regular leg. When a person takes a step, upon striking the ground, their leg absorbs energy that is then released by the ankle, like a spring, as the leg moves forward to take the next step. Artificial limbs utilizing old technology only provide a twenty percent return in energy compared to a real leg. The carbon-graphite foot being designed for me was a major improvement, however the pseudo-ankle still didn't offer the same spring and energy of a real leg.

One of my design suggestions was to glue the sole of a boot onto my artificial foot so I wouldn't have to deal with the weight of a full boot. In addition, I requested they drill a hole through the foot so I could attach various forms of gear to it, such as snowshoes and crampons.

The climb began to take over my life. I awoke each day at 6:00 a.m. and planned until I left for work. After work I exercised from 6:00 to 8:00. Later in the evenings I continued planning into the morning hours, often 1:00 or 2:00 a.m.

Asleep or awake, my mind raced. I wondered what I should be doing next. I pondered what I might need to learn more about. And I was very concerned about my ability to get everything done on time.

To find peace and comfort I turned everything over to God, and continued to hold on to my faith.

A whole new world opened up to me. I found myself talking with business executives, and being interviewed on news and local talk shows.

"Why are you doing this?" they asked.

"I want to show that people can overcome whatever obstacles they face in life," I explained. "It's more than just climbing mountains. It's about dealing with whatever life hands you by placing your faith in God."

I explained the business side of the climb so people would understand this wasn't a wild-eyed project with little planning. The words I needed to convince people to take the risk and put their money in me came very naturally. I realized the more I leaned on God for direction, the more smoothly things worked out.

The exciting part was, it was happening. It was really happening.

We needed a name for our expedition. Whit, Lisa, and I decided on *Summit America*.

Lisa developed a marketing plan for *Summit America*. She needed a promotional logo, so she, Whit, and I sat around my kitchen table drawing different design ideas. After hours of doodling, we walked to a Mexican restaurant on the island hoping to find inspiration in a fresh atmosphere.

Finally, on one of their napkins, we came up with a design we all liked.

Lisa went directly home and created it on her computer.

The next day we ordered one hundred forty-four T-shirts to be printed up. We decided Whit and I would earn money for the project by selling them around the country as we climbed.

Lisa decided to go freelance, so she quit her job at the textile company. This enabled her to do a variety of tasks in preparation for the climb.

There was so much to do and so little time to do it. I poured over the highpoint guidebook trying to figure out our route and determine how fast we had to move to set the record.

A few nights before I left for the climb, Lisa and I walked down to the dock. Standing at the end of the pier, we prayed together. We both knew how important prayer was for the success of the venture.

However, we weren't only praying for the success of the expedition, we were also praying for my safety. Everywhere we went, people offered to pray for my safety.

Deep down I feared for my life, especially on Denali.

When I shared these thoughts with Lisa she assured me, "God has been in this thing right from the beginning. I know He'll carry you safely through to the end."

The media attention was fantastic. It helped get word out about what I was trying to accomplish.

As Whit and I prepared to leave, a newspaper reporter from one of the newspapers Lisa contacted did a story on the climb. The Orange County Network Television and radio station KNX 107 in Los Angeles did the same. The front page of the Metro section of the *Orange County Register* carried our story the day we set out on our journey. On the way to the airport, for our flight to Oklahoma, we heard my voice on the radio discussing the climb.

As I settled into my seat on the plane I recalled the events of the past few days. The most memorable and exciting moment occurred the night before we left, when I finally received my new leg.

The Flex-Foot Reflex VSP was everything I hoped it would be. When I took my first steps I felt a thrill with the realization it didn't hurt. It was made of lightweight materials and had shock absorbers built in, which meant my stump didn't have to take the abuse it did with the other prosthesis. I could move about more freely and less painfully.

I asked if it would hold up to the abuse it would receive throughout the expedition, to which the engineers replied, "Give us a call when you get back and let us know."

"Great! So I'm basically your guinea pig?" I asked.

"Yep!" they grinned.

It wasn't the answer I hoped for, but I understood they couldn't make any promises considering all of its new technology.

As I looked out the window of the plane, I realized I felt physically, psychologically, and spiritually prepared for the climbs. I knew as long as I stayed focused on God while approaching each task, I could succeed.

Once at my parents' home in Oklahoma, Whit and I put a camper shell on my Dad's red Ford pickup and loaded up our supplies. With a final good-bye, we began the adventure of a lifetime.

The official clock for the record started on the summit of the first high point and ended on the summit of the fiftieth one. To break the record we had to climb all fifty in less than one hundred one days.

Heading north, we began the drive which would take us to all of the lower forty-eight states – over twenty thousand miles.

On our way to our first high point in Nebraska I felt the fog of city life lifting from my head. No ninety-mile traffic jams and smog. The open fields and fresh air set the mood for a glorious beginning: Buffalo grass waving in the sunlight; carefully defined fields of early wheat; and endless blue skies with wispy clouds fading to the horizon.

Nebraska's high point, Panorama Point, is aptly named. The view is expansive. With an elevation of 5,426 feet, it sounds like it would be a decent hike. The truth is it sits in the middle of a grassy field.

The U.S. Geological Survey places a marker at the high point of each state, which is measured by the location's elevation above sea level. Therefore, while states such as Nebraska have a high point that is more than 5,000 feet above sea level, the elevation gain for hikers to reach the "summit" is practically non-existent because they begin their ascent from virtually the same elevation.

On the complete other end of the spectrum are summits like Denali. It sits at 20,320 feet and has an elevation gain of 13,120 feet, meaning climbers begin their ascent at 7,200 feet above sea level. Climbs such as these can be extremely strenuous, not only because there is such a substantial elevation gain to conquer, but also because the trails leading to the summit sometimes take climbers over a number of smaller mountains en route to the top.

While breathing in the view from Panorama Point, Whit and I looked at one another. We reached our first high point. We knew it was time to start the official clock. The gravity of what I was about to do was setting in. Though it wasn't a heavy feeling, it made my stomach do a couple of flips.

From this simple summit we were beginning our quest. "The journey of a thousand miles begins with one step," I reflected quietly.

I smiled as I recognized I was, quite literally, living the legacy of this wise, ancient Chinese proverb.

We hurried back and hopped into our car to continue our journey.

Next, we traveled north toward South Dakota's 7,242-foot Harney Peak.

On our way there, just outside of Hot Springs, South Dakota, the sky darkened. Rolling black clouds billowed in the sky. Thunder roared. Bolts of lightning illuminated the terrain in a ghostly light.

Whit peered out at the approaching storm clouds. "Looks like we won't be sleeping outside tonight."

Lightning flashed too near our vehicle for comfort. "Probably not," I muttered.

The rains came – thunderous, pounding rain. During my years in Southern California I forgot what real thunderstorms were like. Our windshield wipers fought to keep ahead of the downpour. We drove slowly, following the dotted white line down a corridor of pine trees. Granite rocks jutted out from among the trees.

I rolled down my window and inhaled the exhilarating clean pine scent. "I love it!"

By the time we pulled into the Harney Peak trailhead parking lot, the rains slowed to a drizzle. I caught a glimpse of a rainbow forming in the east.

I leaped from the car and scanned the patches of blue sky above the peak. "Do you think we should risk it?"

Whit grabbed his backpack from the back of the truck. "Sure, why not?"

I strapped on my waist pack, grabbed my walking poles, and headed down trail number nine, breathing in the clear, clean air as I walked with my new climbing leg.

At first, the trail was muddy, but the ground quickly absorbed the rainwater. It felt amazing to be amongst the fresh smell of rain with the wind whistling through the trees.

Whit and I established a climbing routine. Whit liked to climb solo, so he would either hike ahead or behind me, and would continue this way for miles.

At one point I heard someone approaching me from behind. I turned, expecting to see Whit catching up with me. Instead it was another climber who looked to be in his early thirties. Upon introductions he commented on my artificial leg. I told him about my goal to climb all the high points in the United States. We talked as we hiked, learning about each other's lives. Though he was youthful, he had a worn look to his expression. I asked him what he did for a living.

"Right now?" Dullness washed over his eyes. "Right now I'm not doing much. I'm trained as an engineer. Until a few months ago I worked for a major chemical company back east." He went on to explain that, until recently, he spent his life buying into the money-based dream of happiness. What he found was the deeper he plunged into that world, the emptier he felt. "I obediently went to college and received my degree, and got a job, in a field I didn't like. But it paid well, which I thought would make me happy. But the fatigue finally got to me, so I gave it all up and headed for the hills." He smiled slightly as his hand gestured to the scenery surrounding us.

He kicked a pebble out of the pathway, and my heart went out to him. I knew what it was like to long for a sense of purpose; to desire to make something of a life turned upside down.

I shared some insights I had gained through the years. I told him about the events leading to my amputation, and how I learned happiness comes from being true to your purpose and following who you are. Well-meaning family and friends may try to define what that should be for us, but ultimately we have to follow our own internal guidance and dreams. If we don't live that purpose, we are depriving ourselves and the world of the amazing gift we were created to live. We are depriving the world of our greatness, and the world needs it. I encouraged him to use his time hiking to get quiet within himself and listen for his answers.

When it was time for us to go our separate ways, his demeanor was markedly changed. He shook my hand and thanked me.

As grateful as he was for our conversation, I was equally grateful. For a number of years I suspected the tragic events in my life, and the deep internal spiritual searches I'd done as a result, held some meaning and purpose. I was beginning to think it was because they would give me a platform by which I could help others in a very unique way.

Whit caught up with me at the top of the peak. At the base of the stone lookout tower we read the plaque honoring Dr. Valentine T. McGillycuddy, the first white man known to reach the summit. We shot some photos of the beautiful scenery – mainly rocks jutting out of the pine forest – from the top of the tower.

As we were taking in the view, two young women in their late twenties joined us. They too were from California, and had decided to leave their city life for some adventure. After having some fun joking about the vast differences between southern California and mountain life, we said our goodbyes and wished each other well.

Whit and I hiked back to the car and headed north toward Bowman, North Dakota, which is approximately thirty-seven miles from North Dakota's high point, White Butte.

During our drive toward Bowman, Whit suddenly burst out laughing. "Look at that!" he said, pointing into a field.

There, in the prairie grass, sat a kitchen stove with its oven door wide open and a sign next to it that read, "Open Range." I appreciated the display of humor we saw throughout our travels.

As the evening approached, the torrential rains fell once again. We arrived in Bowman after 11:00 p.m. It had been a long six hundred miles since 5:00 that morning. We found a hotel and checked in for the night.

The next morning I pulled on my cargo shorts and a *Summit America* T-shirt. All of my clothing and gear bore our expedition name or logo of one of my sponsors: PacifiCare, NovaCare, TEC, Flex-Foot, the NorthFace. I was grateful beyond measure for what they each did to make this expedition possible, but looking in the mirror sometimes made me think of NASCAR.

White Butte, like many of the high points, is on private property. While most land owners are supportive of those going to the summit, it's important for climbers to be aware of their various requests. This one asked highpointers to let her know when they'd be climbing on her property.

We had a nice conversation with her as we all talked outside her trailer home. We heeded her warning about rattlesnakes.

"They're everywhere!" she cautioned.

Whit and I read many locals refused to climb there because of the inordinate number of rattle snakes, so this didn't surprise us.

The rains of the night turned the trail to a muddy, slippery, soggy mess, but again I was impressed with the solitude I experienced on the mountain.

After reaching the 3,506-foot summit, we returned to Bowman, cleaned up, and headed south toward Iowa's 1,670-foot high point.

At the time of my climb, Iowa's high point sat in the middle of a farmer's private property, and was one of four unnamed high points in the United States. When the farmer passed away a number of years later, the family sold the land to the county, which named the area Hawkeye Point.

We stopped for lunch on our way there and I called ahead to ask permission of the property owner. I explained who I was and what we were doing. "So you won't mind us trespassing on your property?"

"Of course not. It's no problem," the farmer's wife, Mrs. Sterler, assured us.

"We'll be coming in quite late tonight," I warned.

"That's fine. We enjoy highpointers, and we wish you the best."

I thanked her and hung up the phone. We continued our journey south.

Whit and I took turns driving while the other slept. I drove through quiet little towns and vast fields of grain. While I drove, I reviewed our progress. It felt good to think about the fact that we'd checked off five high points in two days, and I knew when we hit the eastern states we'd be checking them off even faster.

I slowed the truck to a stop near the farmhouse. It was pitch black outside. We hiked up the slight slope between the farm buildings to the water trough. I felt goofy standing in a barnyard in the middle of the night having my picture taken. But there, on the trough roof, was an Iowa license plate – HIGH PT.

We considered throwing our sleeping bags on the ground and sleeping right where we were, but decided to drive farther north to a KOA campground in Minnesota.

At 3:00 a.m. we pulled into the campground, located a camping spot, threw our bags on the ground, and got some much needed sleep.

We awoke at 6:00 the next morning. After a shower and breakfast, we loaded our gear and drove east past Minneapolis. Turning north onto Highway 61, which runs parallel to Lake Superior, we appreciated the tranquil blue water on our right and the rolling green hills on our left.

Eagle Mountain – 2,301 feet high – is the high point of Minnesota. We battled an infestation of mosquitoes on our way to the summit. The marshes and ponds which had been formed by the spring runoff provided the mosquitoes with a perfect breeding ground, and our sweaty bodies provided the lunch. There was no escaping them. We walked as fast as we could across boards laying over the water.

We met one highpointer along the way who was carrying an ice ax. Why he'd carry an ice ax when there was no possibility of snow, Whit and I couldn't imagine, and thought it was very odd.

Once we reached the summit, the swarm of mosquitoes circling our heads discouraged us from talking for very long, so we took our photos and sped back to the truck.

Things were coming along great until that night. The bug spray I used for protection against the mosquitoes proved to be more of a threat to me than the bugs. While trying to fall asleep, I found it hard to breathe, like I was having a panic attack. The next morning I awakened feeling jumpy and light-headed and still couldn't breathe well. My throat was swollen, as were my ears, which looked like cauliflower. I was concerned because I wasn't sure what was going on. It occurred to me it might have something to do with the bug spray, so I drank water and took a shower. Thankfully, it took care of the problem.

From there, we headed for Michigan's high point, Mount Arvon, which stands at 1,978 feet and is located on the state's upper peninsula.

It was recently designated as the high point of Michigan. Modern surveying efforts created a situation of rapidly changing topographical measurements. Several mountains of similar height held the coveted "state high point" status over a short period of time. If another mountain was designated as the high point before we completed our fifty climbs, we would have to come back to summit the new high point.

The first part of our eight-hour drive took us back on Highway 61, and Whit and I drove in silence, watching the magnificence of thunderstorms crossing the expansive lake.

We parked the truck and hiked along a logging road to the top, rather than using the normal hiking trail.

Once we got to the top, and were ready to take our typical summit pictures, we realized there was no vista to photograph. It was so overgrown that foliage blocked the views, as well as a majority of the sunlight. Our pictures could have been from any forested area had it not been for the high point marker the geological survey placed there.

Next was Wisconsin's Timms Hill – 1,951 feet. We climbed the lookout tower at the summit and watched an orange and red sunset with a young couple who had been hiking behind us. We shared our personal challenges and goals with each other. They were finishing college and had dreams of starting a family.

I could tell they were apprehensive about the future, so I told them not to let obstacles hold them back. "Never lose sight of your faith in God and the abilities He has given you, because with them you honestly can overcome anything. I'm living proof," I smiled.

Whit and I arose early the next morning and headed south past dairy farms and green pastures to the Wisconsin-Illinois border.

As we passed a county fair in southern Wisconsin, I wished I had time to stop and stroll along the midway of spinning rides, screaming teenagers, hucksters, and junk-food stands. But we had high points to scale and a record to break. I still couldn't help but feel a little wistful as I caught a glimpse of the nostalgic scene.

We stopped to sleep in the small town of Scales Mound, Wisconsin. Finding a Little League ballpark on the outskirts, Whit unrolled his sleeping bag on the top of a picnic table, while I slept on the grass in left field.

MORE THAN MOUNTAINS

I climbed into my bag, folded my arms at the back of my head, and gazed up at the myriad of stars in the velvety black sky. Feeling the warmth of a friendly, small, all-American town, I drifted into a peaceful, satisfied sleep.

CHAPTER NINE

Mosquitoes, Gnats, and Toenails

The ranger's stories are swirling in my mind as I leave the station. I know I have to hold on to the hope and faith I can make it. I must give it my best shot. I've come too far to give up now.

I call Lisa to check on last-minute arrangements for media coverage. We are counting on them to be our ally in getting the message out, which will bring the financial rewards our sponsors expect for investing in the project.

"An NBC/CNN news team will document your landing at Kahiltna Glacier," she assures me.

"Awesome. Thanks Lisa." I pause, reluctant to break the connection with my friend, business partner, and contact to the familiar Southern California world. "I guess I better go help with the equipment. We have to be ready the minute the weather breaks."

Lisa senses my reluctance. "Be careful Todd."

"You too. After all, more lives are lost on the Los Angeles freeway each year than on Denali," I tease.

"Not in avalanches or hidden crevasses, though," she quips. I sense her hesitation as we say our good-byes. I wait for her to hang up before disconnecting on my end.

Phone calls to Lisa became a big part of the journey. One of the most exciting ones came the first week.

"Todd, you're not going to believe this!" She was so excited I thought she'd leap through the phone lines. "I want you and Whit to hear this together." Whit and I put our ears to the phone. "You know the T-shirt

73

stand I set up on Coral Avenue here on the Island? Yesterday, after sitting there for fifteen minutes with no sales, I prayed, 'God, I'll stay here five more minutes. If you want us raising money this way, let me sell some T-shirts.'"

She stopped to catch her breath. "Immediately a couple came by with their three-year-old daughter and bought three shirts. Just as I put their shirts in a bag, an older man jogged by. Noticing the stand, he turned to see what I was selling. You're not going to believe it!"

I could picture her eyes dancing with excitement.

"I told him about your life, and what you are trying to accomplish. I told him you are trying to prove to people we all have a strength within us more powerful than any challenge we face, and with it there's no limit to what we can achieve. The man asked me how much money it would take to complete the climb, so I told him $50,000."

"And? And?" I couldn't believe she was taking so long to tell me what I hoped she was getting ready to say.

"And the man said, 'Call me tomorrow at my office. My name is John Shanahan, and my number is 1-800-ABCDEFG. I'll write you a check.'"

"What?" My voice must have scaled from bass to high soprano.

"I couldn't believe it. I asked him if this was for real. He assured me it was. The couple who just bought the three shirts witnessed the entire conversation, and the dad interjected, 'Congratulations. You just made a $50,000 sale!'"

I sat stunned, with the receiver glued to my ear.

"So today I contacted Mr. Shanahan. Within an hour he had me in his office asking for details on the climb. I explained it all to him, and he pushed the button on his intercom, 'Sue, make out a check to Todd Huston for $50,000.' Within minutes, I had the check deposited into the account!"

"So who is this guy anyway?" I asked. The phone number seemed strangely familiar.

I heard a delightful giggle at the other end. "The CEO and founder of *Hooked on Phonics*. Mr. Shanahan lives right here on Balboa Island. Can you believe it?"

When I got off the phone a wave of emotion overwhelmed me. Once again God had supplied exactly what I needed. In my mind I joked with

Him about the pattern I was starting to see, and let Him know I was grateful for it.

Whit and I talked excitedly about our future climbs as we drove toward northwestern Illinois.

Curious cud-chewing cows lined the fences as we drove along the dirt road to the Illinois high point, Charles Mound, which sits at 1,235 feet. It is on the border between Wisconsin and Illinois. In the 1800s, when pioneers made their trek west, White Oak Fort was located on Charles Mound to protect Kellogg Trail, an old stagecoach and wagon route.

This was yet another high point located on privately owned farmland, so we walked up the driveway to get permission from the landowner. A dog rounded the corner of the barn, barking. An older woman in a housedress and Mother Hubbard apron opened the front door. The dog trotted over to her, protectively growled, and then hid behind her skirt.

I smiled to myself at the thought of how surprised the dog would be if he bit my leg.

She watched me through narrowed eyes as I explained our purpose for being there. "All we really need is your permission to walk across your land to the marker, then we'll be on our way."

"It'll cost you five dollars, for upkeep and all," she stated abruptly.

Upkeep? I couldn't imagine what she meant considering there were cow patties lying everywhere.

Not wanting to waste time discussing the matter, I reached into my pocket for a five. She took the money, stuck it in the pocket of her apron, and scurried back inside the house, taking the dog with her. When the door closed, I heard a definite click of the lock.

I turned to Whit and grinned, "Obviously she's not into highpointers."

He scratched his head and smiled, "Guess not."

We climbed the gates, dodged through cow dung, and ran past a group of tombstones – lost graves from covered-wagon days – to the high point.

After taking the necessary snapshots, we hurried back to our car and headed southeast toward Indiana's high point. It was unnamed when we climbed it, but has since been dubbed "Hoosier Hill." It sits in the middle of a field, marked with a small rock cairn and a steel pole with a sign attached reading, "Indiana's High Point – 1,257 feet."

Then it was on to Campbell Hill in Ohio, another small high point at 1,549 feet. It is located in the middle of a schoolyard.

We parked at Hi Point Church and hiked a half mile to Hi Points Joint Vocational School. The students were gone for the day. We found the gate to the fenced-in yard but it was locked. Whit and I scrambled over it and walked up the hill to the flagpole, which marked the high point, and took our pictures.

From Campbell Hill, we headed toward 5,344-foot Mount Marcy, the highest point in the state of New York. Finally, a mountain with the elevation gain to give us a true summit experience.

We spent the night near Cleveland, then drove through a corner of Pennsylvania and up to Niagara Falls.

In spite of our rush, we took time to tour the Falls. I'd seen them before, but Whit hadn't, and was amazed at their size. We read a sign telling of people who'd ridden down them in barrels, and agreed they were crazy.

After clicking off miles and chunking change into toll plazas along the New York Turnpike, we headed north from Syracuse toward Watertown, then east along Route 3 through the hills of the Adirondack High Peaks Region. We drove the last several miles to the Mount Marcy campground in drizzling rain.

Our guidebook told us the mountain's Indian name is Tahawus, meaning "cloud splitter," and in 1901 Vice President Teddy Roosevelt rushed down the mountain when he learned President William McKinley died.

Though it was late when we arrived, we stopped at the Adirondack Mountain Club lodge and asked the ranger about the climb and a place to sleep.

"It's a strenuous hike," he warned. "14.8 miles to the top and back."

I asked him about the trail. "How long will it take to climb to the summit?"

"Well, that's hard to tell. If you find you're only partway up the mountain and half your day is spent, you'd best turn around and come back down."

"That's not what I mean. If you're worried about my artificial leg, you should know we're out to set a world record. We're on our way through the eastern states before we climb Denali." I didn't mention one of my toenails was black from an earlier climb.

"Oh, well, then I guess Marcy won't be too big a challenge for you fellows. You might want to watch out for bears, however."

"Bears? What do I do if I meet one? Climb a tree?"

The ranger chuckled. "Make a lot of noise while you're on the trail. They typically run away before you get to them because they don't want to see you any more than you want to see them."

The next morning I led the way up the Van Hoevenberg Trail, setting a fast enough pace to be out of sight of Whit and the truck before long. All along the wide, well-marked pathway were lean-tos and rest areas. At all the campsites people had their food tied up in trees to keep the bears away. I chatted with a number of day hikers I met.

After a few miles, the trail became rocky and steep and split in various directions, some trails for hikers and others for cross-country skiers. As the route grew more rugged, I worried I'd taken the wrong path until I saw a blue mileage marker and knew I was still on the correct trail.

Though I was grateful to see the marker, I did not like what it told me. It read 7.4 miles, which seemed like a very long hike to the summit. This was the longest one-day hike I'd ever done, and my toe was really starting to bother me.

This hike was hard. I crawled up dry creek beds, crossed rushing streams, and hopped from boulder to boulder trying not to fall. If I fell my prosthesis could get caught in between the rocks and snap in two, leaving me stranded until someone came along.

Whit caught up to me and his timing couldn't have been better. As he arrived I tripped over a rock and fell face first. Instinctively, I threw my hand out in front of me, and when I opened my eyes I was two inches from having a nose job. Whit helped me up so we could keep going.

We made our way the final distance to the summit in the stillness of the fog and drizzle. On the way we stopped to rest beside a beautiful waterfall trickling softly with fresh spring runoff.

As can be true when climbing to higher altitudes, the weather on the summit was very different. We were chilled by the stiff, frigid winds.

"Sure glad it's not winter," I said, as I tightened the drawstring to the hood of my nylon jacket.

Massive cloud formations billowed above our heads as we huddled beneath a couple of giant boulders to pose for pictures.

Worried, I eyed the storm clouds blackening the sky. "We'd better hurry back and drop below this." Whit agreed.

We hurried back down the mountain. I led the way, with Whit following a comfortable distance behind.

My stump throbbed from the long climb as salty sweat burrowed into my wounds. I stopped to rest, relieve the pressure, and allow blood to circulate through the area. This caused a burning sensation that felt like rubbing sandpaper on an open wound. I talked with other hikers as they passed while I massaged my swollen limb.

The rest of the way down, every half mile or so, I stopped to loosen my artificial limb and let blood circulate into my stump.

Whit caught up with me at one of the lakes. After checking to make sure I was alright, he hiked on. When I was able to continue, I counted each step and mentally divided them into miles to the camp. The last mile felt like ten, but I made it to the end of the trail and found my dad's truck.

I went to a pay phone to call Lisa, but got the answering machine. At the beep, I said, "I am really sore. Marcy was a tough fifteen-mile hike, but I promise I'm doing OK."

A long, hot shower soothed my leg and restored my spirits. I felt good about what I accomplished that day, however I knew it was nothing compared to what awaited us out west.

The ranger invited us to a barbecue that evening, but we had to refuse. We still had a long drive to Vermont's high point, Mount Mansfield.

After a very welcomed night of sleep at a fellow climber's bed-and-breakfast, we drove to the Mansfield trailhead. Grabbing our jackets and water packs, we hiked up the 1.4-mile trail to the summit at 4,393 feet, swatting mammoth flying bugs and pesky gnats with each step.

Along the way I talked with a woman named Patty. She was a nurse who, like me, was going through a painful divorce. She'd married an alcoholic without knowing it.

"It devastated me."

I nodded. "I know how you feel. That's exactly how I felt after Jessie left. Something I realized is important is letting go of the resentment. You have to forgive. It's not hurting him when you feel anger toward him, but it is hurting you, and it is holding you back from being the light and love you are."

She grimaced. "I know. However, right now…"

"No excuses," I joked with her. "It's the heaviest load you can put on your back. Let it go. You'll be amazed at how free it makes you feel."

She thanked me for our talk as we hiked off the mountain together.

Next, Whit and I headed for Mount Washington in New Hampshire. By the time I found a phone to let the ranger know we were on our way, the toll road up the mountain was closed for the day. However, when the ranger heard what we were doing, he offered to get us a special pass.

"Be sure to come by the office to pick it up when you arrive," he told me.

We could see the impressive 6,288-foot mountain for miles before we reached the base. Occasionally a cloud obscured the peak. In the guidebook we read hikers everywhere considered it dangerous due to the weather fronts that often collided at the summit. In 1994 alone five people died hiking it.

The rules of highpointing do not require that a person hike to the marker if a road is available, so we drove the narrow, winding toll road instead of hiking the summit trail or riding the cog railway. Sheer drop-offs prevented us from driving too fast over the alpine terrain.

Once we reached the summit, overcast skies and blowing winds threatened, so we took our photos quickly.

We checked out the tram, which was built in 1869 and is the oldest cog railway in the world. Next we made our way to the lodge and looked through the gift shop and restaurant. Though the building had a more modern, rounded look on the outside, it had a rustic charm on the inside.

From Mount Washington we drove to Maine's Mount Katahdin, which stands at 5,268 feet.

Climbing Katahdin's strenuous three-and-a-half-mile trail would be a one-day climb, like Mount Marcy. The summit is called Baxter Peak, and is the northernmost point of the Appalachian Trail, which runs from Maine to Georgia.

We found a place to park by a lake to sleep. I was tired and knew I needed to be ready for Katahdin. We threw our sleeping bags on the ground and were about to sack out for the night, when the gnats found us.

Buzzing in my ears, crawling across my forehead, crawling into my nose, the pesky creatures persisted in spite of the mosquito netting covering us.

Whit called dibs on the truck's cab. The only other enclosed place was a nearby outhouse. In desperation, I threw my gear into the truck and plodded over to it. As I opened the door I was practically knocked over by the potent stench. Though the thought of it absolutely turned my stomach, I was resigned to the realization this was the best place to sleep. I sat with my back against the wall and forced myself to shut my eyes and rest. The smell was easier to deal with than the gnats.

We began our summit hike along the Appalachian Trail early the next morning. The fresh forest air was heavenly after sleeping all night in a toilet. However swarms of mosquitoes took over where the gnats left off the night before.

Hill after hill we climbed, sometimes steep, sometimes gradual, until we broke into the clearing above the timberline. We hiked up steep boulders to get over a rocky ledge and onto a large plateau.

Throughout the entire hike the swarms of bugs were militant. Stinging black flies, which were a cross between a mosquito and a horsefly, bit through our long-sleeved shirts. Their bites drew blood and left huge, painful welts on our arms, legs, and necks. We wore our heavy shirts despite ninety-degree temperatures.

We finally reached the summit, however didn't feel as satisfied as we had on other summits.

Whit looked around and growled, "Fine! We made it. Let's take the pictures and get out of here!"

I couldn't have agreed more. Sweaty, thirsty, exhausted, and with streamlets of blood running down my good leg, my ears, and my neck, I continued swiping at my attackers.

"This is miserable!" I moaned.

On the way back down the mountain, I stumbled onto the secret for warding off Katahdin's insect population. I soaked in every stream I crossed, and once I was drenched, the bugs left me alone. Though it was a relief, it barely minimized my incredible discomfort.

By the time I climbed into the truck at the trail head I ached all over. My toenail looked worse, my stump throbbed from the pain, my ears looked like overgrown cauliflowers again, and I was so thirsty I was beginning to feel light-headed.

We stopped for cold drinks at a little general store outside the park. I considered finding a pay phone to make a call, but didn't have the energy. My stump felt as if someone stuck a thousand needles into it, so while Whit was in the store I removed my prosthesis and turned the heater in the truck to high. I'd discovered that, in lieu of a soaking bath, the heater eased the pain in my stump.

Whit came out to the truck and opened his door. A gust of hot air blasted him in the face.

"What? Are you crazy? I can't believe you have the heater on in ninety-degree temperatures," he exclaimed.

"The heat helps. It really helps," I winced.

He climbed into the truck, rolled down his window, and closed the vents. "I suppose I can survive the heat until we find a suitable motel."

I appreciated his understanding.

We drove through the warm countryside with the heater blasting while drinking cold Snapple.

I could barely walk from the truck to the office by the time we located a motel. The thought of putting my artificial leg back on made me cringe, so I hopped from the office to my room. Once inside the room, I called Lisa, then my mother.

When I told my mother how much my left foot was hurting, she urged me to have it X-rayed. "You might have broken it," she warned.

I looked down at the blackened toenails. One was barely hanging on. I promised to oblige.

Whit drove me to a hospital in Bangor, where I asked for an X-ray. The nurse on duty in the emergency room asked how I'd managed to injure my foot so badly.

"Climbing mountains."

Her eyebrows arched in surprise, "Mountains?"

"Yep," I grinned. "My buddy and I are out to break the current world record by climbing to the highest points in all fifty states in the least amount of time. We have a good chance of doing it if I haven't messed up my foot."

"Isn't it a little unusual for a man with your disability to climb mountains?"

"That's the whole point. I want to prove challenges in our lives don't need to keep us down. With faith and determination, we can do whatever we set our minds to." And then I added, "Of course, no one said it would be easy."

She smiled, nodding her head as I spoke. "That's terrific. So many people come through this hospital despondent and giving up on life. I'm glad to meet someone who doesn't allow their limitations to keep them from pursuing their goals."

The X-rays came back a few minutes later. Everything looked fine except the blackened nail dangling from my toe. I knew the nail would continue to be a problem, especially if it didn't heal before I climbed the western states.

"I hope this works," I said to Whit.

Taking a paper clip, I straightened the wire, heated one end with a butane lighter from our camping stove, and cut the nail and peeled it away from my toe.

"That's disgusting," Whit shuddered.

It was a good thing he wasn't around for my amputation.

CHAPTER TEN

Delaware Danger to Texas Heat

The wings of the red Cessna 172 dip low over the Kahiltna Glacier as our pilot prepares to land on the expansive glacier field at the base camp. Crevasses line the edge of the landing area. The plane's skis scrape over the icy surface as we skate to a stop.

Adrian taps me on the shoulder and points out his window. "There she is."

I open my eyes and take a second to get my bearings. I'd been sleeping. I'm exhausted and nervous.

It's impossible not to be stunned by the size of the mountains surrounding us. Colorado's mountains look like molehills next to these.

And then there's Denali. It dominates everything in its wake, and is as gigantic and beautiful as I imagined it would be. A large lenticular cloud caps the summit. My heart is racing.

I check my watch, tap it, and give it a little shake to make sure it's working. 5:15 p.m. How can it be so late? We spent much of the day waiting for the weather to break so we could land on the glacier. Due to the heavy cloud cover, the pilot was forced to return to Talkeetna, where we waited for a window in the storm front before returning. This was our second attempt. Finally we got the break we were waiting for, and were able to fly in.

There's no turning back now.

The base camp is at 7,200 feet. Groups of tents surrounded by ice walls cling to the glacier like tiny colonies. Climbers bustle about in the evening twilight making last minute preparations for the grand coming with the morning. A group of climbers, their sunburned faces tired and worn and their beards scraggly, stand at the edge of the landing field waiting to board the plane so they can finally return home.

Every glimpse I catch of the majestic mountain triggers a sense of awe within me. We've climbed some impressive peaks, but this one has been looming in my thought throughout the expedition.

The pilot taxies across the runway to a cluster of people waiting at the edge. Immediately I identify the NBC/CNN news team Lisa promised would be here.

As the propellers whir to a stop I adjust my sunglasses, take a deep breath, and try to look confident in front of the cameras.

Someone opens the door and I step gingerly out onto the glacier and its temporary snow runway. On the flight the pilot shared a story about someone who stepped out of the plane and into a crevasse and disappeared right on the airfield.

A brisk wind whips around the tails of my jacket. I inhale the crisp Arctic air surprised it isn't colder. Reports indicated it is "nuking" at the 17,200-foot base camp near the top, meaning the temperature is forty below zero with a 70-mile-per-hour wind.

I duck under the wing and wave to the camera. A reporter approaches me with a microphone in his hand. Burying my apprehension, I slip into what has become my public persona. Curious onlookers watch as the reporter tosses the usual questions, and I reply with the expected answers.

My confidence grows when he asks, "And what do you hope to accomplish with this climb, beyond, of course, setting a new world record?"

Squaring my shoulders, I smile toward the camera. "More than anything else, I want to send a message to people everywhere that life's challenges do not need to stop them from reaching goals and breaking down barriers. Through determination, and understanding God supplies you with everything you need to overcome whatever life throws your way, you can successfully conquer any obstacle."

However I don't feel as confident as I sound. I'm about to face one of the loftiest challenges on the continent.

After the trip to the emergency room we drove to my Uncle Bill's home outside of Boston and I rested for the next day-and-a-half.

This was the same uncle who was with me during the amputation, and a man I admired. Even in his eighties, this very proper Bostonian gentleman exercised a sharp mind. He was once asked to become the ambassador to Norway. Now he taught history at Emerson University.

A couple of months prior to our visit he suffered a heart attack and stroke, and flatlined on the operating table. I could tell he was feeling a little down because he'd always lived such an active lifestyle and hadn't been able to since his heart attack and stroke. While I wanted to encourage him, I realized there was a fine line between stretching oneself and causing more damage by over-doing. I remembered the lessons I learned the hard way after my injury, when I accidentally pulled out stitches and IV needles.

His son-in-law, who worked for the BBC, was also visiting from England. Whit and I had a relaxing time, laughing and talking and sharing stories with them about recent events in each of our lives.

Early Sunday morning, Whit and I said our good-byes. I eagerly anticipated the easy climbs of the rest of the East Coast and South. I'd have plenty of time to heal. The next major climb wasn't until Colorado.

We headed for Rhode Island's high point, Jerimoth Hill – 812 feet. We were warned by other highpointers about the man who lives at the mouth of the dirt road leading to the high point. While Jerimoth Hill is owned by Brown University, the dirt road leading to the high point runs along the edge of a man's property who isn't fond of highpointers. For some reason, when he sees one, he screams and threatens to call the police. It's been rumored he's taken shots at them as well.

We located the man's big red farmhouse and parked our truck on the other side of a nearby radio tower, 200 yards beyond his property. He'd parked his big tan van across the entrance to the dirt road to keep people from hiking on it.

When we got out of our truck we heard organ music coming from his house.

"It's Sunday morning," I told Whit. "He is probably getting ready to leave for church. I bet he'll be in a friendlier mood than usual."

Being a trained psychotherapist and self-appointed guardian of the reputation of highpointers everywhere, I grabbed the camera from the seat and announced, "I'm going to knock on the door and get his permission."

"Why?" Whit looked at me in astonishment. "We're not going to trespass on his land so why should we bother to ask?"

"Because it's the respectful thing to do," I answered.

Music poured from the open door as I walked up the sidewalk. Whit lingered behind, obviously not as confident in my talents at problem solving as I was. I reached the doorstep and raised my hand to knock, when I paused.

I started getting that spooky feeling you sometimes get when you are in the middle of nowhere and the potential for danger is lurking in the back of your mind. What made me think this man would be any nicer to me than he'd been to the numerous others who had tried to be polite and respectful? Visions of a gun-barrel in my face compelled me to turn around, quickly. I whipped about and ran as fast as I could down the walkway.

"Come on," I whispered as I dashed past Whit. "Let's go! Let's go!"

Whit didn't need a second invitation. We charged across the highway, around the tan van, and up the dirt road. We didn't stop running until we reached the rock cairn representing the high point. I tossed the camera to Whit and doubled over to catch my breath.

"Hurry! Take the picture!" I straightened up and smiled victoriously at the camera.

"Got it!" Whit shouted. "Here!"

He handed me the camera. We switched places and repeated the process.

"Got it!" I stuffed the camera in my waist pack. "Come on. Let's get out of here."

We ran down the dirt road to the parked van. As we dashed across the highway to our vehicle the man came out of his garage. Whit and I ran full speed toward our truck.

Apparently he didn't see us yet, because he strode across the highway and hopped into his van.

That's when it happened. He caught a glimpse of us, obvious hikers with our truck bed piled high with hiking gear.

By the glare on his face it was obvious he intended to prevent us from making the climb.

I chuckled out loud. "We should stay here a while and make him late."

Whit laughed. "Yeah, let the guy think we haven't done the climb yet."

"As much fun as that sounds, we have mountains to climb." I started the engine. "We're out of here."

Whit mused, "Can't you hear that guy mumbling under his breath as he goes in to church? 'Boy, I really showed those guys! That'll teach those highpointers to come around here and bother me!'" The image had me rolling with laughter.

We wasted no more time and headed west down the highway.

We pulled up to a tollbooth along the Massachusetts Turnpike. Our destination: Massachusetts' 3,487-foot high point, Mount Greylock. A reporter and photographer unexpectedly joined us for the climb. I was excited to realize word about what I was doing was getting out there.

The mountain was incredible. It's known to be the most scenic of the eastern summits. It is green and lush, and is classified a Monadnock, which is an isolated mountain rising steeply above the surrounding land. In fact, its beauty is so awesome it inspired Herman Melville to write *Moby Dick*.

At the summit we climbed the ninety-foot granite tower. It is a war memorial built in 1933. We took a few pictures of the villages in the surrounding valley, then wandered through the Bascomb Lodge cafeteria and gift shop.

From there, we dropped down below the Massachusetts-Connecticut border to 2,372-foot Mount Frissell.

Oddly, we had to climb to the top of the Frissell, and back down to a lower elevation, to get to the Connecticut high point. The mountain is shared by Massachusetts and Connecticut, with the actual peak lying in Massachusetts. Therefore, Connecticut's high point is just across the border, about a quarter of the way down the mountain.

"Three mountains in one day. We're doing great!" I grinned at Whit as I handed the camera back to him.

On the way back to the truck I met some elderly climbers who recognized me from photos they saw in a magazine. It was great talking with them. Though they were older, they were determined not to let age stop them from doing the things they loved to do. They were incredibly youthful and happy, and I enjoyed hearing about their experiences. The joy they radiated reminded me of how I felt when I was young and played at the creek by my house.

As I hiked down the mountain, I thought about how kids find such joy in simple things, like nature, yet as they get older they get caught up in the "necessities" of the world – money, cars, country clubs, and other shallow material things. It's a shame age makes some people forgetful of what brings true joy and peace.

This couple, as they got older, found that their appreciation for those childlike joys never left them. In fact, they'd grown stronger.

The relaxing drive between the high points took us past some beautiful countryside. This was the time to relax, before we headed west.

Whit and I passed the time by talking and listening to the radio. Usually one of us drove while the other slept. We had no time to waste if we were going to break the record. Always looming in the back of my mind was the western states, and the ever present concern of Denali.

It was late by the time we pulled into Wilmington, Delaware. Whit and I joked sarcastically about the danger we faced at Delaware's high point – Ebright Road. As its name reveals, it is in the middle of a Delaware street.

Other than running over a center median while turning, we found the 442-foot high point without any trouble.

The next morning we drove to the high point of New Jersey. Whit and I couldn't help but chuckle at its name – High Point. Standing at 1,803 feet, it sits in the midst of a lush 14,193-acre state park. Miles before we reached the high point we could see the two hundred-foot monument donated by a local family in honor of all war veterans. We read in our guide book that the view from the top is impressive, so were disappointed to find it was closed due to renovations.

We proceeded to Pennsylvania where we ate a big lunch in a small Mennonite restaurant before driving west.

We passed tidy little Amish farms where we saw farmers tilling their land with hand plows. Their wives, dressed in black and wearing black cotton bonnets, hung their freshly washed laundry on clotheslines in the back yards. We drove past Amish families seated in coaches painted black, driving their matching sorrels to town, and blue-and-black-clad children swinging lunch boxes on their way to school. It was like stepping back a century in time.

We drove to the top of the 3,213-foot Mount Davis, Pennsylvania's high point, then hiked to the large boulder a few yards west of the observation tower to take our official pictures.

As we drove to our next high point in Maryland – Backbone Mountain at 3,360 feet – I was feeling more confidence and less fear than when I began this journey. I was enjoying the process. I had no idea how much stress I was feeling until now. I enjoyed this new sense of relaxation.

While the summit of Backbone didn't offer the incredible views of other summits, it was very peaceful. There was a gentle breeze blowing around the little bench sitting in the midst of the lightly forested area.

Whit and I hiked back down the hill to the truck and headed toward West Virginia's high point, Spruce Knob.

We drove from Maryland across a portion of Virginia to the Monongahela National Forest and Spruce Knob Recreation Area. We drove most of the 4,861-foot mountain in the truck, however since we'd been driving so much, we both wanted to hike around a few summit trails after taking the necessary summit pictures. Whit took one trail, while I took another.

I hiked out through a clearing of scrub blueberry bushes and stunted mountain ash to a rock overlooking a valley. Perched on top of the rock, I thought of where we'd been and where we still had to go, and the problems still needing to be solved before we returned to the west to climb Gannet, Hood, Rainier. And Denali.

A principle component we needed to figure out was who would be our guide on Denali. My first choice was Adrian Crane, the current world record holder.

But we needed additional support. An experienced climber named Mike, who was a Sergeant in the Army, came highly recommended. The challenge was he could only join us if we had a letter from a high-ranking congressmen requesting the Army grant him a leave of absence. Without this we would have to find someone else. A guy we met climbing one day volunteered to contact Washington's Congressman Lewis who was a friend of his.

"Anything I can do for you, let me know," he offered. I made a mental note to ask Lisa to take care of this.

Our next high points rolled by relatively effortlessly: Virginia's Mount Rogers – 5,729 feet; Kentucky's Black Mountain – 4,139 feet; and Tennessee's Clingmans Dome – 6,643 feet. Then along the Blueridge Parkway to North Carolina's Mount Mitchell – 6,684 feet; some twisting country roads to South Carolina's Sassafras Mountain – 3,554 feet; and Sumpter National Forest to Georgia's Brasstown Bald – 4,784 feet.

When we arrived at the Brasstown Bald summit, the visitor's center was closed and the place was deserted. We looked everywhere for the summit marker but couldn't find it. We had traveled nonstop to check off four high points in one day, and I really needed to use the restroom. Since the only one in the vicinity was inside the visitor's center I decided to walk over to what appeared to be an abandoned log cabin to satisfy my problem.

Right at the moment I began to relieve myself, a woman opened the front door of the cabin and walked out. Seeing what I was doing, she ducked back inside her home.

Embarrassed, and feeling the need to explain myself, I knocked on her door. When she answered I told her we were highpointers, apologized for my honest mistake, and mentioned we were having trouble finding the benchmark.

"Sure, I'll show you where it is." She took us over to a locked gate. "It's right there. If you didn't know where to look, you'd never find it."

"How are we going to stand on it to have our pictures taken?" Whit asked, eyeing the benchmark through the gate.

"I think I know a way." I stretched my leg through the iron bars and touched it with my foot. "There! Take the picture." Then Whit took his turn.

We took some time to talk with the woman. She told us of the events leading to her living on Brasstown Bald.

"After my husband died and my kids were grown, I needed to find a new life for myself. Doing volunteer work at different national parks has allowed me to travel as well as build a new life for myself," she shared.

She talked about the challenge of getting beyond the death of her spouse. "We were married for so many years. I had to fight depression every day that first year after he died."

I was impressed by her strength and resilience. She expressed a great deal of love and joy, and I knew it's how she made it through her challenges so well. She gave us a warm good-bye before we headed back down the mountain.

During the next few days we checked off the high point at Mississippi's Woodall Mountain – 806 feet – and Florida's unnamed high point – 345 feet.

Florida's high point, which has since been dubbed Britton Hill, is actually the lowest "high point" in America.

I was in a joking mood when we made it there, and was tempted to don all of my snow gear for the picture, but it was just too hot and humid.

I loved the view from Alabama's 2,405-foot Cheaha Mountain, the place where the Creek Indian Wars took place in 1813, but hated the humidity.

We met a family there who was in the midst of moving to a new location. The children expressed their fears about making friends and attending a new school. I told them about my accident when I was fourteen, and how I had a lot of fear about what people would think about me and how I would make friends. I told them the biggest lesson I learned was, when we go out into the world with the goal of giving love, regardless of how others see us or treat us, we will end up with some really great people in our lives. I learned I didn't have to worry about what people thought about me. All I needed to do was approach every situation with kindness, joy, patience, humility, and so on. I found the more I did this, the more people returned those qualities to me. And when I came across people who didn't respond positively to me I didn't let it bother me. I treated them just like everyone else, and knew they would someday learn to be the love God created them to be, too.

These ideas really resonated with them and calmed their anxiety. They were a great family, and I knew the children would do well on their next great life adventure.

We slept on top of the high point that night. Fast-moving clouds rolled overhead, occasionally offering us glimpses of the moon. Another peaceful evening.

The next morning we hiked back to the truck and headed north to Taum Sauk Mountain in Missouri, at 1,772 feet, and south to Arkansas' Magazine Mountain, at 2,753 feet.

We spent the night at Jack Longacre's house in Mountain Home, Arkansas. Jack was a lively, talkative man and the president of the Highpointers Club of America. He wrote the highpointers' newsletter and kept the statistics on the climbs.

After a meal of the genuine southern cuisine of beans and cornbread, we shared our clippings and photos with him, and he showed us mementos from the entire history of highpointing. One thing I learned was highpointing started when there were only forty-eight states, and only four people are known to have reached each of these prior to the addition of Alaska and Hawaii in 1959.

The following day we drove near the scene of Bonnie and Clyde's fateful final showdown on our way to Driskill Mountain in Louisiana – 535 feet. The heat was becoming unbearable and we lost our air conditioning in the truck. We decided to climb at night to avoid the heat as much as possible.

The next day we drove in one hundred eighteen-degree heat to the other side of Texas to Guadelupe Mountains National Park. This was where Geronimo, the chief of the Apaches, held out against the U.S. Cavalry.

We spent part of the day sitting in a remote Texas lake trying to cool off while we waited for the sun to set. We then headed up the 4.4-mile Guadelupe Peak Trail to reach the 8,749-foot summit.

It was definitely cooler, but still ninety-four degrees.

We slept at the top of the summit. It was a few feet away from the edge of a 150-foot cliff so we placed rocks around our sleeping bags to keep us from rolling off in our sleep.

We woke up early and waited for the sun to rise. As soon as it cleared the horizon we began racing down the trail. Within a very few minutes the temperature was climbing once again. Already it felt like we were walking in an oven. As we passed hikers on their way to the top, I hoped they had a lot of water for the climb.

We had a date with another high point, a special one this time – in my home state.

CHAPTER ELEVEN

The Real Mountains Begin

On our way to the Kahiltna Glacier ranger's station to check in, we pass clusters of tents scattered across the field of snow. They are nestled inside protective snow walls built to act as weather buffers.

Snow is the mountaineer's friend and foe. Climbers walk on it, sleep on it, slide on it, and cook with it. They melt it to ward off dehydration. They use it to insulate themselves against wind, temperature drops, and unexpected mountain storms. However, they have to protect themselves against blindness and intensified rays caused by the reflection of the sun off of it. These rays can cause extreme sunburns, because they hit climbers from above and below. It isn't uncommon for climbers to get a sunburn inside their nose from the reflection.

Looking down at the well-scarred snow crunching beneath my boots, I marvel at how bright everything is. Though the sun has gone down it is still light enough to read a book.

While Adrian and Whit unload our gear, Mike and I locate the park ranger. She introduces herself as Annie. She is a dental hygienist from New England but spends her summers working as a park ranger for the National Park Service.

She directs us to a campsite and warns us about the weather, "It's deceptively warm right now – don't let it fool you. Temperatures may drop tonight because there's a low-pressure system moving in. But it should be gone by Monday."

We thank her and begin to set up camp.

"Can you believe the number of people here?" I whisper to Mike. "Are they all here to climb Denali?"

"Yep," he answers.

A dusting of snow falls on us as we're setting up.

By the time the cocoa is hot I can feel the mountain's low temperatures in my bones. I cozy the mug between my stiffening hands and sip the hot liquid. Since arriving at the 7,200-foot base camp I've been incredibly thirsty. At this altitude, dehydration is a constant concern.

After eating I decide to get acquainted with the climbers camping next to us. We have some good laughs as we swap stories about our climbing experiences and the events bringing us here.

"My goal is to break the world's highpoint record set by Adrian," I tell them.

"How did you get interested in mountaineering in the first place?" one inquired.

"The organizers of this program called '50 Peaks Project' wanted to show people challenges need not stop anyone from accomplishing their goals. When they didn't get their funding, I decided to go it on my own."

One of the climbers whistles through his teeth. "Good luck, man. That's treacherous terrain up there, even for a two-legged man."

I grimace. "So I hear."

A new surge of energy infused us as we drove north toward my home state of Oklahoma and its high point, Black Mesa, which stands at 4,973 feet. One of the largest mesas in the world, Black Mesa's eighty acres spill into Colorado and New Mexico. Located on the far western end of Oklahoma's panhandle, it was once known as No Man's Land, and harbored bandits and outlaws in the mid-1800s. It's also an archeologist's heaven for dinosaur excavation.

I was beginning to feel quite proud of my abilities as a mountain climber on my way up the mesa, but was quickly humbled when I arrived at the summit to find a group of third- and fourth-graders who were there on a field trip. They were a great group of kids, and I gave them an impromptu talk about my accident and the obstacles I've overcome.

"Don't look at people with disabilities like we can't do anything," I told them. "We all have challenges, ours are just different from yours."

They shared some of their challenges with me, and we talked about the importance of treating everyone with love and respect regardless of the difficulties they are facing.

We signed autographs and posed for photographs on the granite summit marker. They invited us to hike back down the mesa with them. On the way, right in front of me, one of their teachers fell. I calmed the kids as I carefully lifted a rock off her leg. Whit and the other teacher carried her down the steep hill while I led the kids from behind.

"It's a good thing we were here," I said to Whit as we drove to the Kenton Mercantile to register our climb. "I'm not sure how they would have made it down without our help."

We used the phone at the Mercantile to call the park rangers in the western states regarding the conditions of their trails. They reported the snow had been melting rapidly and the trails looked great.

We hopped in our truck and headed to Kansas' 4,039-foot high point, Mount Sunflower. Lightning flashed and thunder roared from the heavy cloudbank to the west of us as we drove. Hail and heavy rain occasionally pounded us, but thankfully the storm never produced a tornado.

The weather cleared by the time we drove to the summit and posed for pictures. In an effort to add some excitement to this high point, Kansans created a unique, six-foot high sunflower constructed of railroad spikes to mark it. Furthermore, in light of historic events that have occurred atop a number of the U.S. high points, these Midwesterners showed their sense of humor with an engraved metal plaque that read, "On this site in 1897, nothing happened."

Exhilaration coursed through me as I drove north from Mount Sunflower to the Kansas-Colorado border. We'd checked off the thirty-eighth state in less than thirty days. Colorado's Mount Elbert – 14,433 feet – would be the thirty-ninth. The best part of it was we were weeks ahead of the record. "I think we just might make it!"

"Huh? What?" Whit looked over at me in surprise.

"We're going to do it! We're going break the highpoint record!"

We hiked up Mount Elbert's eleven-mile primary route in the early morning because summer afternoons on the mountain often bring showers and thunderstorms. We didn't want to get caught on one of the mountain's exposed ridges in freezing rain or snow. We were especially wary of being there during an electrical storm. A climber on Elbert had recently been struck by lightning and killed.

As I climbed the final 1,000 feet, the elevation made me a little short of breath, but otherwise I felt strong. Once on top, the view was spectacular. Mountains filled the view as far as the eyes could see.

Climbers dub mountains above 14,000 feet as "14ers." There are sixty-seven of them in the contiguous US, fifty-three of which are in Colorado. Several of these giants command the view from atop Mount Elbert.

The air was crisp and I could feel a slight breeze blowing around me. It was hard to leave this breathtaking view, but I had a goal and needed to get down the mountain to continue on my journey.

On the way down I found traces of mountain sheep. I hoped to spot at least one, but it wasn't to be that day.

I marveled at the fact that I had just climbed my first real mountain. I felt completely rejuvenated – like I could conquer the world, and was ready to take on whatever challenge a mountain threw at me. My leg and toe had healed sufficiently and didn't hurt. I accelerated my pace, swinging my arms and singing made-up songs as I hiked. Fortunately nobody was around to endure the torture of my voice – it would have definitely tainted their hike.

A practice I had taken up when we started this expedition was silently and humbly thanking God at the end of each climb before preparing for the next one. At the bottom of Elbert, I closed my eyes, took one final breath of the fresh mountain air, and said my thanks.

Back at the truck, I studied the road map trying to decide which route would be the best to get to New Mexico's 13,161-foot Wheeler Peak.

Wheeler Peak lay in Carson National Forest, and driving the winding roads there took most of the next day. The trailhead began in one of the Taos Ski Valley parking lots, so we pulled in, found a place to pop our tents, and got some sleep.

We began our ascent at first light, hiking the Blue Lake trail to the three-foot high stone and mortar monument atop the peak's high point. We took our photos and headed back down a shorter, but steeper, route.

One thing I was always wary about, but had yet to experience, was an encounter with a bear. It's one of the biggest dangers for hikers. Since

1990 there had been ten known fatalities in North America resulting from bear attacks. I tried to go down the mountain quickly, but had to step carefully because the trail was littered with loose gravel and rocks. I was getting close to the bottom of the mountain when I looked up and saw what appeared to be a bear headed straight toward me. I knew I couldn't outrun it, especially with the hill being so steep and unsteady, so I froze in my tracks, hoping it wouldn't notice me and turn off the trail. I stood there for what seemed like an eternity, barely breathing, with my heart racing and adrenaline coursing through my veins. And I was praying. Man, was I ever praying!

All of the sudden, a family came up behind the "bear" and called out to it. It turned out to be their family dog – a dark, hairy, 200-pound Newfoundland.

I heaved a huge sigh of relief and made my way down to the family and their dog, Jack. They were thoroughly entertained upon hearing my account of what just happened. Their kid's faces lit up with huge smiles at the thought of their sweet, playful dog scaring someone like that.

We all shook hands, I patted Jack on the head, and I continued on my way. When I arrived at the truck I was still feeling the effects of the adrenaline rush, and was glad to be back in the car where I could sit and unwind.

We drove into Taos, where I called Lisa for an update on media arrangements for Arizona's high point.

"We got him!" she shared excitedly. "Congressman Lewis wrote the letter arranging for Mike's military leave. He can join you in Wyoming!"

"That's fantastic news, Lisa! Thanks." With Mike along on Denali we had a real shot at the record.

From Taos, we headed west to Flagstaff, and north to Arizona's high point, Humphreys Peak. It is the tallest of a group of extinct volcanic peaks known as the San Francisco Peaks. Like Alaska's Denali, this 12,633-foot mountain is sacred to nearby Native American tribes.

Sarah Jane, a reporter from a local paper, met us in the field below the mountain and shot a few photos. I asked her if she'd like to climb the mountain with us.

"Me? No way! I could never climb Humphreys."

I smiled. "Well, you know, part of my purpose for climbing all fifty high points is to encourage others to overcome their limitations. Maybe I can help you, too."

She shook her head in disbelief. "I don't know." I spotted a glimmer of desire in her eyes.

"Aw, come on," Whit urged. "We'll help you."

She took a deep breath. "OK, I'll give it a try."

We maintained a constant pace up the mountain. At one point, my artificial leg slid between two rocks and I fell hard. However, by then I'd fallen enough to realize it's simply part of hiking.

With a little help and a lot of encouragement, Sarah Jane made it to the top. She couldn't believe the view. To the north we could see the Grand Canyon's North Rim. We turned around, and behind us was a stunning view of the desert mountains near Phoenix.

We wrote our names in the register and took some pictures.

"I did it! I did it! Yes!" Sarah Jane shouted for all to hear

We took our time going back down to the trailhead so we could bask in our success a little longer.

Sarah Jane thanked us for the unexpected adventure and we all went on our way. It was time for us to head north to Utah.

The five hundred-mile ride took us past some ruggedly beautiful desert scenery. When we arrived in Salt Lake City, Kirsten, a friend of Sarah Jane's and a reporter with a local newspaper, met us on the capitol building steps and interviewed me. Rick Porter, from the *50 Peaks Project*, also met us there.

The *50 Peaks Project* had been a vision and dream of Rick's, and I knew he was disappointed he hadn't been able to get funding together for it. I appreciated his original motive in putting the project together, which included a message similar to my *Summit America* message. I decided to invite him on the Utah climb, and asked him to do us the honor of videotaping it, offering to pay him for his time. The look of gratitude on his face was the only confirmation I needed that this was the right thing to do.

After spending a relaxing evening touring Salt Lake City with friends, Rick invited us to his home to meet his wife, Natalie, and their children.

We spent a lovely evening together.

The next day we drove to the starting point of our Utah highpoint climb. Oddly, we had to drive into Wyoming and then double back to Utah's High Uintas Wilderness area of the Wasatch and Ashley National Forests. The guidebook said hikers usually take two to five days to make the strenuous 28.8-mile hike to the top of 13,528-foot Kings Peak. We camped at Henrys Fork Basin campground and started early the next morning so we could get as far as we could on our first day out.

The weather was warm enough I could wear cargo shorts and a T-shirt, however packed a fleece jacket and windbreaker for the cooler evening. As an added safety measure I stuffed down pants and a jacket in my pack in case of a storm.

Whit went ahead. I set a slower pace to protect my stump from the strain created by the more difficult mountains. I came to a stream and sat down on a rock to rest, when I looked up and saw a Boy Scout troop emerging from the woods to cross the stream.

One of the boys turned and looked at me curiously; then he noticed my artificial leg. "Hey, you're the guy with one leg who's climbing all the mountains. I saw your picture in the paper last night."

I grinned. "That's right. I'm the guy." Lisa's publicity work was paying off. We were beginning to be recognized almost everywhere we went.

A second Scout walked closer to me. "Everybody's talking about you."

"Oh?" I asked.

"Yeah, you're some kind of hero," he replied.

The other boys gathered around the rock. Questions flew for the next hour.

One boy asked, "Were you ever a Boy Scout?"

"Yes. I am actually an Eagle Scout and loved every minute of my scouting days. I always enjoyed going camping in the wilderness with my friends. Plus, everything I learned in Scouts has been very helpful to me through the years. Our leaders taught us a lot about life skills, such as character building and honesty, in addition to the obvious things Scouts need to know, like safe hiking and rescue techniques."

We joked around for a while longer before I resumed my climb up to 11,888-foot Gunsight Pass. It was given this name because if its V-shape, similar to what you see when you look through the gun sight of a rifle. I caught up with Whit there and we stopped at the top of the pass to wait for Rick to catch up with us.

"Since you have to move slower, maybe you should go on while I wait for him," Whit suggested. "You can find us a good camping spot."

"Good idea." At the foot of the hill I checked the map to figure out which was the right trail. The shorter trail went through marshy glacier terrain covered with underbrush. The longer trail was higher and dryer. I chose the higher trail.

At Anderson Pass I looked back and saw Whit on the trail behind me, but Rick was nowhere in sight.

"Where's Rick?" I questioned.

Whit cast me a wry grin. "He's a half-mile back. He says he's blown out and can't go another step."

I glanced around us. Small clumps of bushes dotted the reasonably flat surrounding area.

I recommended, "We could camp here for the night."

"Good idea. I'll go back and get Rick." Whit hiked back to where he left Rick and brought him to our chosen campsite.

We ate our dehydrated food as the sun set. With our sleeping bags laid out on the ground, we watched as a canopy of stars filled the clear night sky. I took out a book on astronomy I purchased in Taos and tried to identify the constellations. Before we went to sleep we talked about the next day's climb. We would summit, then hike straight back to the trailhead.

After breakfast, Rick set out ahead of me so he could get some good video sequences of me climbing to the top of the mountain. He bounced about, taking video footage of me as I hopped over the rocks above the timberline.

Climbing up the ridge to King's Peak, the rocks became boulders. Once at the summit, he got footage of me signing the register and gazing out thoughtfully over the beautiful valley, and towering peaks and plateaus surrounding us.

I strolled over to the marker to read the plaque telling some of the history of the summit. "In honor of Clarence King (1848-1901), an

American geologist who . . ."

Hearing a shuffle behind me, I turned, expecting to see Whit. "Hey, Whit. Did you know…"

"Hi." A honey-blond woman in her twenties with a great smile on her face and a black lab by her side paused a few feet away from me.

"Hi, yourself." I couldn't help but return her warm smile.

Whit and I at the summit of Maine's high point, Mount Katahdin.
With the beautiful scenery came black flies, mosquitoes, heat,
and humidity. It was one of our most miserable climbs.

Always a welcome sight. These USGS metal markers would often be
placed on the highest points. I personally jumped on every one I saw.

Many high points, like this one in Georgia, are marked by historical signs.

The lowest high point in our country—in Florida.

Without Lisa's faith and hard-working support, the Summit America expedition would never have made it.

Whit and I celebrated reaching the high point of Massachusetts. Mount Greylock, a war memorial, sits at the top of the mountain.

Delaware's Ebright Azimuth sits right in the middle of a busy street. It may not be the most dangerous high point, however dodging traffic to get this shot proved a bit unnerving.

This is why they call them the "Smoky" Mountains.
A beautiful, if foggy, panorama in Tennessee.

A foggy day at the summit of
North Carolina's high point.

On my way up Mount Rogers, Virginia.

A typical Eastern high point — a rock surrounded by trees.

A grouchy neighbor tried to block the path to Rhode Island's high point with his van. We snuck past before he saw us.

I met this group of lively students on Oklahoma's high point, Black Mesa.
This large mesa has steep cliff sides. On the way down, the teacher slipped and broke
her ankle. I led the kids the rest of the way while Whit helped carry the teacher down.

Even on the highest mountain in Texas, Guadalupe Peak, it was hot.
We climbed at night because it was 118 degrees that day.

Eagle Mountain,
the high point of Minnesota.

Hundreds of mosquitoes enjoyed munching
on us as we crossed these wooden
walkways on our way up Eagle Mountain.

At the highest point in Kansas, Mount Sunflower.
The sunflower is constructed out of welded railroad spikes.

One of the more dangerous climbs, Borah Peak in Idaho,
had a knife's edge ridge with a dizzying drop-off on both sides.

Barbara and I (and Kona) resting at Island Lake
during the climb of Gannett Peak in Wyoming.

Though it's the middle of summer, Mike, Barbara, and
I hiked through snow near the summit of Gannett Peak.

Gannett Peak had the most
beautiful scenery of any climb.

Camping on Froze-to-Death Plateau on the way to Granite Peak in Montana. The rangers warn climbers to watch out for blizzards on Froze-to-Death, even in the summer. The rock wall shelters help protect climbers from wind and snow.

From Tempest Peak, we could see our destination— Granite Peak. We climbed from the slope on the left.

Whit, Mike, and I at the summit of Granite Peak.

I made it to the top! Nevada's Boundary Peak sits right on the border of Nevada and California. The Sierra-Nevada Mountains in the distance made a beautiful sight.

The Flex-Foot VSP with a Vibram boot-sole glued to the bottom. This leg carried me every step of the way!

I was always impressed with the beauty of the mountains as well as the people I met. Mount Wheeler, New Mexico.

My now traditional victory pose on top of Mount Whitney at sunset. It is amazing what God can do with us when we have faith in Him and the abilities He's given us.

Whit, Fred the "copy cat," and I
at the Timberline Lodge before
we started up Mount Hood.

Using ski poles helped me on the climb up
the awesomely beautiful Mount Rainier.

Fred, Lisa, Whit, and I stopped to
encourage a young handicapped girl and
her family on our way to Mount Hood.

Mount Whitney, highest elevation in the lower forty-eight,
where I slept higher than anyone else in the United States that night.

The Denali team—Whit, Mike, Adrian, and me.
The beautiful red chariot would carry us up to the glacier.

My last meal?
I am not sure I even tasted the pizza,
but Mike and Adrian were more relaxed.

We flew through One-Shot Pass
on our way to Kahiltna Glacier.

Whether or not they spoke English, many climbers supported and encouraged me along the way.

Without being roped up, it would be foolish to stand next to this beautiful, but deadly, crevasse.

We headed up Kahiltna Glacier, a vast expanse of ice and snow, loaded up with gear and pulling sleds. As strange as it sounds, we worked to avoid sunburn and frostbite at the same time.

Here at Denali Pass, a recent accident claimed the life of another climber. Mike rests on his ice axe while making the summit approach from the 17,000-foot camp.

A typical group camp site or tent city, crowded with climbers. The snow walls offered protection from the weather.

Resting between climbs to get acclimated. I took a few minutes to read a book.

Not your usual ranger station. This tent at the 14,000-foot camp served as the ranger station and offered assistance and information for climbers.

Roped together, the team
climbed the West Buttress.

We dug out a camp site and space for
a kitchen. No one left the immediate
camp site without being roped up.

"Thank you, God!"
I am standing at the summit of
Denali, the top of North America!

The team poses for a sponsor shot with
the "Hooked on Phonics" T-shirts.
It was too cold to change into one.

There were many congratulatory banners as we arrived at Mauna Kea.
Hawaii's volcanic high point is in the background.

The final climb leads up
Mauna Kea's moon-like surface.

More personal congratulations from
a beautiful Hawaiian at the luau.

CHAPTER TWELVE

Froze-to-Death Plateau

As the raucous banter flies back and forth between the seasoned mountaineers, my own thoughts are fixed on the adventure that lay ahead.

When it's finally time to get some sleep, I climb into my sleeping bag, roll over onto my side, and whisper into my recorder, "I choke up when I think about what God is doing for me. Why me? So many people are praying for me. It is both frightening and overwhelming."

I click the button on the recorder and set it on my pillow.

I stare at the semi dark dome of nylon arching over my head and think about my purpose for climbing the mountain. I think about the people who will hear my story and be inspired to climb their own "mountains."

Then I remember the horror stories of avalanches, rock slides, whiteouts, and crevasses.

I squeeze my eyes shut. "God, this is yours."

We awaken to blue skies and brilliant sunlight. After a breakfast of oatmeal, hot chocolate, and hot cider, the four of us rope up and walk six miles up the glacier to get a feel for the landscape.

Sunlight sparkles off the icefalls. The glacier's crevasses reveal its scars, creating a kaleidoscope of whites and deep blues surrounding the outcroppings of rocks.

Every direction we look we see lofty mountains. However, beyond the beauty of the glacier, beyond the host of lesser peaks, one can feel the presence of The Mountain. Always The Mountain.

"It's so high!" I crane my neck to study its splendor. Rising almost three miles above us, The Mountain takes my breath away. All of the superlatives I know pale in the shadow of the Great One.

As though inside a majestic, revered cathedral, the conversations on the glacier are spoken in hushed tones. I talk with the other climbers, eager like me to begin their ascent. I speak with the sunburned, beat-up climbers coming off the mountain, almost too exhausted to reply.

"It's rough up there," one admits as he lumbers past me.

Rough up there. The gravity of his words are setting in as we walk back to our campsite.

The blonde woman smiled again.

"You're the guy in the news who's out to break the record for climbing the fifty peaks, aren't you?"

"Guess so," I extended my hand. "I'm Todd Huston."

"My name's Barbara." She glanced down at her black Lab mix dog. "And this is Kona."

"Hi, Kona." I patted his head. He rewarded me with a lick. "Are you a park ranger or something?"

She laughed. "No."

"Well you obviously spend a lot of time outdoors. You're legs look like steel."

She tipped her head to one side and laughed. "I do spend a fair amount of time outside. I'm a mountain guide at Telluride."

"What do you do when you're not guiding groups up mountains?"

"Well," she hesitated. "I do a little skiing."

I eyed her curiously. "Why do I get the feeling there's more to this story than you're telling?"

"OK, I'm a member of the U.S. Women's Extreme Ski Team." I found out later she was actually Barbara Scheidegger, the Extreme Ski Champion.

"Really? So what are you doing up here on King's Peak?"

She waved her hand out over the rock ledge. "The same thing you are – climbing mountains."

I introduced her to Whit and Rick. The four of us talked for a while about the mountains we had climbed, and the ones we were looking forward to climbing.

"I go from here to Gannett Peak in Wyoming. I hear it's a strenuous climb." Barbara shifted her weight from one foot to the other. Kona sprawled out at her feet for a nap.

"That's where we're heading," I said. "How many are on your climbing team?"

"Just me."

"Wow," I frowned. "You might consider having other climbers with you on that one since it's more of a technical climb. Why don't you hike with us?"

"Really? You or your partners wouldn't mind?"

Whit's eyes widened. "No way would I mind."

I laughed. "It would be nice to have someone new with us. We're starting to bore each other."

We took the steep route on the west side of Anderson Pass down the mountain. Rick and Whit went ahead so they could pack our gear for the next climb, while Barbara, Kona, and I took our time, especially over the area with loose rocks. I jumped from rock to rock praying I wouldn't fall and end up several hundred feet down the mountain. When I landed on one rock, I jumped to the next before the first one had a chance to slide out from underneath me.

She told me she was struggling with a deep sense of loneliness lately. "Maybe it's because my dad died last year and I feel so empty without him." She paused, "I know you're a psychologist. What do you think?"

I smiled. "The psychology only got me so far. I've found the real answers come from somewhere else."

My confidence in my message and ability to help others was solidifying throughout this expedition. In addition, we had quite a bit of time to talk on the long hike down. We were able to get into a deep discussion about losing a loved one and the loneliness that tends to accompany it. "When someone we love passes on, we still carry their light and their love in our hearts. In that sense, they are still very much with us, and they never leave us. We are a representation of them in everything we do. And I believe they would want us to carry that light and love into the world and joyfully share it with others, to continue to make the world a better place. Then we find the connection we had with them isn't about time and space, it's about oneness in the heart. Which is why sometimes we can feel disconnected with someone standing right next to us, but completely connected with someone half-way around the world, or even with someone who's passed on. It's not that you are empty, because you still have that love within your heart. You just aren't able to express it in the way you are used to, which, in this case, was with your father. So, now your challenge is to figure out how you're going to express it in new ways, which will nurture that love to grow into something even greater and stronger. This gives you the opportunity to bless others and increase the expression of love within you. And the coolest part is, when we are living that love, and our motive is to bless others with it, we find it's impossible to feel lonely."

When I was finished sharing these ideas with her, I looked over to find a tear rolling down her cheek. The gratitude in her eyes as she turned to look at me said it all. I patted her warmly on the back and we continued on our journey.

We spent the rest of the hike chatting about our lives – our families, her boyfriend, and funny mountain climbing incidents.

She also told me about her skiing career, which began when she was twenty-one. Since then, in addition to her skiing, she did a little modeling. "I've been on the cover of *Ski* magazine and done commercials for VISA." She looked at me, smiled, and said, "This is the Scheidegger smile."

"Magazine or television?"

"TV. Maybe you've seen the VISA ad where the blonde jumps out of a helicopter, lands on an extremely difficult run, and skis down the mountain?"

"Yeah! That's you?"

She shrugged and laughed. "Some of us will do anything for money."

I asked if I could see her portfolio and her publicity scrapbook some time.

"You're really interested, aren't you?" She sounded surprised. "You're not asking just to be polite."

"Of course! I think what you've done is amazing!"

When we got to the place we agreed to meet Whit and Rick, they were nowhere in sight. Exhausted, I found a rock beside a stream and sat down. My legs ached. This had been the longest hike since Mount Marcy in New York.

Barbara tossed her backpack on the ground. "Are you hungry?"

105

"Hungry? Are you kidding?" My stomach was growling as I spoke.

"Then you rest your leg and I'll cook us something." She pulled a camp stove out of her pack and went to work. Before long, Kona was eating his meal while we talked and ate ours.

A half-hour after twilight, Whit and Rick arrived. They had taken a different trail, which turned out to be quite a bit longer. By the time we hit the trail once more, we needed to use our headlamps.

Back at the parking lot, Barbara and Kona headed for her Mazda pickup and makeshift camper, while Whit, Rick, and I threw our sleeping bags on the ground. It was a long, tiring day, so I had no trouble sleeping through the aches in my legs.

The next day I rode with Barbara to Jackson Hole, Wyoming, where she planned to meet her boyfriend and I had arranged to meet Mike. Whit and Rick followed behind us in my dad's truck.

I looked through Barbara's portfolio and was impressed. This girl was driven, which explained her success on and off the mountain.

We hit Jackson Hole late that afternoon. As we approached the parking lot where Mike and I planned to meet, I saw this no-nonsense, military looking guy with chiseled features and remarkably muscular arms. There was no doubt this was the mountaineer I'd heard so much about.

"There he is." I pointed toward Mike.

Barbara parked her truck and we all got out.

"Mike," I called and waved. "Over here."

It was great meeting him face-to-face. I introduced him to Barbara. With their common interest and experience in climbing, she and Mike hit it off right away.

Mike glanced down at his watch. "If we're going to get our gear for tomorrow's hike we'd better hit the mountaineering store."

We bought the necessary food and supplies and headed for a pizza parlor for dinner. While everyone ate pizza I placed a call to Hawaii for a radio interview in anticipation of my climb to their high point, Mauna Kea. It was to be the final high point of the *Summit America* expedition.

With the phone call out of the way, we dropped Barbara's truck off at her boyfriend's house and headed toward Wyoming's Gannett Peak, which sits at 13,804 feet and is on the border of the Bridger and Fitzpatrick

Wilderness areas. To scale it, we had to hike 20.2 miles to the top, then back down again.

After we pitched our tents in an open field a ranger stopped by. The main bit of information he needed to tell us was grim. "Watch out for a skier who we're presuming died in an avalanche a few months ago on Dinwoody Pass. We told him not to attempt it because we knew the avalanche danger was high, but he ignored us. All we've been able to locate so far are his poles and one ski."

A reminder that, as good a time as we were having, this was not a game, and we needed to be extremely careful.

We set out on the trail before dawn the next morning, our headlamps lighting the way. It wasn't long before the early morning light revealed the striking beauty around us. A variety of wildflowers dotted the fields and forest pathways. Five miles up the trail I paused at Photographer's Point to admire the gorgeous view.

While we were there we met a botanist and his hiking partner. He told us about the wildflowers indigenous to the Rocky Mountains. "Bluebonnets, asters, and elephant ears. You're here at the most perfect time to appreciate them."

I gazed about me, nodding in agreement. "It's like walking on a multicolored cloud."

I spent the night in my tent to avoid the bugs while the others slept in the open. The next day Barbara, Rick, and I relaxed on the rocks like lizards, while Mike and Whit scouted the route to the summit.

The following day it was time for our summit attempt. Kona stayed at the campsite because his paws did not have the necessary traction for this.

Our hike took us to the top of Dinwoody Pass, where I caught my first glimpse of Gannett Peak. It didn't seem like it was that high, however I quickly realized how wrong I was.

When looking at a mountain, its sheer size can give the illusion it is much closer than it appears. In this case, we had a number of valleys and smaller peaks to scale before reaching Gannett's summit.

After going through one of the valleys, we came to Dinwoody Glacier Moat, which is an ice field on the outskirts of the glacier. Once we were in the center, we looked around, and what we saw brought chills to my spine.

We were in the middle of a spider web of crevasses.

Snow covered some of them, forming what looked like little snow bridges. We had to get through the area quickly, while it was early and the snow bridges were still frozen. Once the sun hit the area, the hard snow would turn to mush, and hiking across would be very dangerous.

At the top of Glacier Gooseneck Pinnacle, Whit pointed toward one of the many peaks in front of us, stating, "There's the summit over there."

"Are you sure?" I looked at the peak he was pointing out, then at the one to its left. Both peaks looked the same to me.

Mike came up behind us. "Yeah, that's the one – the one to the right."

I shook my head. "The one on the left seems higher to me."

"Well," Mike reasoned, "we'll be able to tell when we get a little closer."

He sped on ahead while we hiked down the glacier, where three experienced rock climbers caught up with us.

"Can you tell us which of those two is Gannett Peak?" I asked.

"That one," the oldest man answered, pointing toward the peak on the left.

About then, Mike called back to us, "It's the one on the left. I can tell by the trail." We all laughed.

Stepping up the pace, we soon came to a bergschrund. A bergschrund is a very large crevasse running parallel to the mountain. It is found where the glaciers are born. Since glaciers are rivers of ice moving slowly down the mountain, there is often an area where the main section of moving ice separates from a smaller section that is stuck to the mountain.

Upon seeing the bergschrund, Mike said, "Time to rope up."

I roped up with Barbara. Together, we inched our way up the snow bowl, constantly aware of Rick's whirring video camera. The winds whipped around us, which made my sweat feel icy against my skin.

As we got closer to the top I understood why some climbers make it this far and decide not to attempt the summit. Walking across the snow to the peak reminded me a little of walking on a balance beam. On one side was sheer rock face, and on the other a steep angle of snow and ice leading to a cliff.

After carefully balancing our way across the snow, we made it to the summit.

Looking at the mountains surrounding us, and reflecting on the twenty-mile hike to reach the peak, I decided this was one of my favorite summits. The valleys, lakes, and wildflowers made for a breathtaking journey.

After resting for a few minutes and visiting with some of the other climbers, we started down. This is always more difficult, in part due to the muscle fatigue.

Mike and I roped up for the trip over the bergschrund. When my artificial leg postholed, I knew I was in trouble. But I didn't know how much trouble until I poked my ski pole into the snow where my foot had gone down. It punched straight through into a crevasse that looked to be up to one hundred feet deep.

My mouth dropped open as I stared down the hole next to where I stood. My senses quickly returned and I leaped back, doubly thankful we'd taken time to rope up. We decided to walk along the edge of the bergschrund instead of on the glacier itself. Beneath our feet we saw water flowing under the ice cap. When we finally stepped onto solid rock, I breathed a sigh of relief.

We kept a steady pace throughout the rest of the climb, despite the swelling in my stump and the soreness in my good leg.

I took Whit up on his offer to carry my water bottle, which was a mistake. I started getting extremely thirsty and he was too far ahead to come back to me. Fortunately, Mike waited for me and helped me create water from the snowfield.

When I got back to camp I was shaking from the physical exertion of the climb. I took two Advil, crawled into my sleeping bag, and waited for the pain to stop while I rested. Whit knocked on my tent and handed me a nice dinner, which helped ease the pain.

After a good night's sleep we headed for base camp and our vehicles. We stayed in Jackson Hole for an extra day so I could rest and get some business done. It also gave all of us the opportunity to treat ourselves to hot showers and a nice meal.

We said goodbye to Barbara and Kona the next morning. I could tell Mike really appreciated having someone with us who also understood climbing. They became great friends throughout the climb, and Barbara helped us see the softer side of Mike. He was very gentlemanly and considerate toward her, quite the opposite of the stiff, military demeanor he wore with us.

Next on our agenda was Granite Peak, Montana's 12,799-foot high point, which stands in the Absaroka-Beartooth Wilderness. If any mountain in the lower forty-eight could keep us from making all fifty climbs, this was it. It is known for its exceptionally steep rock climbing and bad weather. There are places throughout the mountain that leave climbers very exposed, and if the weather doesn't cooperate, they find themselves with no choice but to abort their summit attempt.

Our drive took us north past the Grand Tetons, through Yellowstone National Park and its renowned geysers, and then farther north along Beartooth Pass highway in Montana. This is one of the most scenic highways in North America, with its deep, lush valleys and cascading mountain peaks.

Once at the base of the mountain, we hiked from the trailhead to a clear, calm lake shimmering with the reflection of the surrounding mountain peaks.

By the time I reached it I was by myself. Whit and Rick were quite a distance behind and Mike was well ahead. I came across some climbers who had seen a bear.

"He left the camp and headed that direction," one of them said, pointing in the direction toward which I was going. I made a lot of noise to ward it off as I continued my hike.

The trail suddenly got steeper and rockier as it switchbacked up the mountain. The difficulties of this climb began to set in. I thought about the mountains that lay ahead and began feeling discouraged. After the strenuous hike at Gannett, my stump was aching and sore, and carrying a sixty-pound pack on my back up this steep trail was aggravating it even more. Furthermore, I was worried about the bear.

I began to seriously second-guess the whole expedition.

"What does anybody care?" I spoke out loud, though there was nobody to hear me. "I could fall off the mountain, get eaten by a bear, get caught in an avalanche, or freeze to death, and nobody will even know the difference."

I stepped off the trail as I sincerely contemplated the option of shutting the whole thing down and going home.

Then I was reminded of the reason I began this journey.

I thought about all of the people in the world who would benefit from hearing my message about overcoming challenges. I thought about the times I had communed with God and felt He was leading me to make something of the tragic events in my life – to use them to show people there is nothing they can't overcome.

The old feelings of yearning to help people began swelling up inside of me again.

I looked up, took a deep breath of the fresh air, and stepped back on the trail with a renewed sense of purpose.

Not long afterward Whit and Rick caught up with me, and I told Whit I needed some help. "Carrying this pack is killing my stump, and I'm not sure I'll be able to make it to our destination if I have to go on like this."

Whit's kindness really shined through at that moment. He offered to carry some of the things in my pack, which lightened my load immensely. The camaraderie and selflessness within the climbing world is unparalleled. The well-being of the team is as critical as the well-being of the individual.

The three of us continued on to Froze-to-Death Plateau. The U.S. Forest Service warns people about the snowstorms possible at any time on this plateau. There is nowhere to gain cover, so freezing to death, as its name indicates, is very plausible. Fortunately for us, the weather was clear and comfortable as we hiked it.

We encountered a field of large, jagged rocks miles long. As I hopped from rock to rock, I was constantly guarding against the possibility of slipping and falling.

After nine hours of climbing, Whit, Rick, and I made camp. Mike was still ahead of us and we didn't know where he was. We would have continued on to look for him, but the setting sun was casting shadows across the rocks and it was becoming increasingly dangerous.

The next morning our mission was to find Mike. We headed toward the top of Mount Tempest where we finally spotted him.

"Where were you guys?" he asked, obviously not thrilled we left him alone on the mountain. We explained to him why we stopped, and though he was irritated, he understood and was glad to see us.

With a major rock climb looming, I suggested we take a day off so I could rest. Mike spent the day training Whit and Rick in technical climbing. They learned how to belay rope across rocks.

Though it was pitch dark, we began our hike down the side of Tempest Mountain at four the next morning. We had to start early to reach the summit that day. We next climbed the ridge connecting Tempest with Granite Peak. We roped up when we reached the boulder area. After testing the slings, we used them and the webbing left by guide groups, to climb the boulders.

Occasionally, as I belayed across a sheer drop, I glanced down at the thousands of feet of air below me and congratulated myself on not panicking. Several times we heard a minor rock slide in the distance. Of course, no rock slide is minor if one of them hits you in the head.

Our next task was scaling the huge rock walls to the Crux, the hardest part of the ascent. Then came the Key Hole, which is two rocks perpendicular to the mountain with another slab on top, creating a hole you have to hike through to reach the summit.

Finally, approximately one hundred feet beyond the Key Hole, was the summit.

"Yahoo!" I shouted as I stamped my boot on the benchmark. "We made it!"

The four of us reveled in our accomplishment. It wasn't an easy one, but standing here and taking in the views, we all agreed it was well worth it.

I was the first to rappel down the rock on the return trip, a nerve-racking experience when the end of your rope is dangling in 3,000 feet of air. There's no one to protect you if you slip off the end. I slowly let myself down onto a ledge by traversing twenty or thirty feet to the right. I undid the rope, and set it for Whit.

I loved this climb. Since upper body strength was paramount to both the ascent and the descent, I was faster than everyone else. All of those months of weight training and ocean kayaking paid off.

Suddenly, above me, Whit slipped. Instinctively, I pulled the rope tight. Whit got another hold and was safe.

"Glad you think fast!" he shouted down to me.

He soon joined me, and the others followed without incident.

At the Crux, we rappelled down another thousand feet onto a ledge eighteen inches wide where we anchored in. From there Mike led the way down the ridge to a snow bridge.

"Kodak moment!" he shouted halfway across. Then he snapped a picture of me at the edge of the bridge.

"AAHHHH!" The shout behind us was followed by clanging and banging. I whirled around to see Rick falling on his backside down a thousand-foot slope of snow and ice.

Rocks and snow tumbled down ahead of him. Then, as suddenly as he started sliding, his heel caught on a rock and stopped him.

"Don't move!" Mike shouted. He ran to the edge, surveyed the danger, and made his way down to help Rick to safety. Whit and I just stared at each other in amazement. Another close call on Granite!

The dangers of the mountain put us in a solemn mood as we followed the cairns back to Froze-to-Death Plateau. Cairns are manmade stacks of rocks helping climbers know where to go when the path isn't apparent.

The sky was dark and the wind whipped fiercely around us as we started across. Then the storm broke. Lightning bolts struck all around us. With sheer cliffs on each side, there was nowhere to run or hide. We were at the mercy of the elements. Nothing like a few lightning bolts to get someone praying.

Fortunately, most of the storm hit a peak to the north of us. In spite of my concerns I enjoyed the dramatic light show.

At the edge of the plateau I spotted three climbers heading up. One of them shouted, "Is that you, Todd?" I squinted my eyes, trying to identify the man. Who would know me at 12,000 feet in the remoteness of Montana?

"It's Ron. Remember me?" It was a pastor from Oregon I met on another high point.

"Hey Ron! How are things going?" I stopped to talk with him as the others went on. He was a very interesting person who was easy to talk to. I needed to move on, so we talked about what our plans were for the next couple of days. When we realized we were both going to be climbing

Idaho's high point next, we agreed to meet there.

Once at the bottom, we packed up to head for Idaho. We stopped in Bozeman, Montana, to meet with my friend Fred, who was in town visiting friends. It was great to see him again.

Upon hearing of the events leading to this expedition, and learning of the journey thus far, Voni, the friend Fred was visiting, was also very supportive. "God is using you, Todd. He's given you a tremendous opportunity to influence many people's lives, and He's putting you in a position to do so."

She spoke with complete conviction. I had heard it from Lisa and family members, but coming from a complete stranger, someone I just met, was even more inspiring to me. It strengthened my resolve to complete this expedition.

We drove across Montana to Idaho where we could climb Borah Peak. Though Borah's summit is 12,662 feet, not long ago it was only 12,655 feet. In 1983 there was a 7.3-magnitude earthquake that raised the elevation of the peak an unheard of seven feet.

Two reporters, Dan and Mike, met us when we arrived at the campsite. They were happy to use this interview as an excuse to get out of the office.

That night I came across an older gentleman who planned to climb alone, and invited him to join our team. We crashed for the night, anticipating the climb the following day.

Ron and his buddies arrived just before dawn, excited about doing some serious climbing. We set out for the day.

Beginning with the trailhead, Borah proved to be an extremely steep hike. As if this wasn't difficult enough, the mountain threw us some other obstacles. Just above 10,000 feet, we reached a knife-edge ridge. With 1,200-foot drop-offs on both sides, we were fortunate to have great handholds.

Then we reached Chicken Out Ridge. This passage is so steep many climbers get discouraged and don't make it the final 1,000 feet to the summit. With our experiences on Gannett and Granite we scaled it with relative ease.

The snow bridge to the summit was easy to walk across, but one slip would send a person a long way down the mountain. We saw ski poles lying farther down the slope. Hopefully the skier escaped injury. This was a graphic reminder of the care climbers need to take with each step. Taking chances could lead to a loss of time, unnecessary exposure, or injury.

As Ron and I hiked, we talked about our faith in God and what it meant to have Him actively involved in our lives.

"You know Ron, I've got to get a book out on this project. There is a higher purpose to everything I've gone through, and it can be used to help others. A book would be the perfect way to do that."

He thought for a few seconds, "I have some contacts in the publishing industry who may be able to help you. If you'd like, I can make a couple of phone calls when I get back."

We continued our hike to the summit, talking about ideas for the book. Once we were there, we registered the climb and headed back down the mountain. We said goodbye at the trailhead.

"I'll make the call right away," he promised.

"Great! Thanks!" I smiled and waved.

As I walked to the truck, I reflected on the events of the last week. I realized if I had pulled the plug on this expedition, like I considered doing on Granite, I never would have met up with Ron.

Ron did, in fact, help me get *More Than Mountains* published, and it has helped me share my message with a wider audience.

I'm grateful my resolve to get back on the trail, and finish my journey, led to a book that has helped so many people struggling with their own challenges. Furthermore, the book has been written into a screenplay, and if the movie is made, it will be able to help even more people.

That day on Borah Peak the lesson was clear to me to never give up, regardless of how challenging life seems. We never know the things going on out there preparing the world for the greatness that lies within each one of us. The important thing for us to do is to show up each day and give life our best. We don't need to question where our hard work will lead, we just need to continue our work, having faith our greatness is continually blessing ourselves and others, sometimes in ways we may never know.

Most of the mountains now behind us, we knew we had a viable chance of breaking the record.

But it was nearing the time to face Denali.

The record, the success of the whole expedition, would ride on my back to the top of that mountain.

All along the way, when interviewed by the press, I said, "Denali will be the big challenge. You have to respect every climb, large or small, but that mountain is a whole different ballgame."

Over dinner that night, fear and anxiety gripped me as we discussed the next leg of our journey – Rainier. It would be our warm-up for the Great One.

CHAPTER THIRTEEN

On to Rainier

When I called Lisa that night she asked for my projected climbing schedule so she could coordinate the media coverage.

"A representative from *Hooked On Phonics* wants to be at the Mauna Kea climb in Hawaii," she reported.

The mere mention of Mauna Kea, the last high point of the expedition, produced butterflies in my stomach. I dreamed of that summit for so long.

In Spokane we stopped at an REI store and spent another $1,200 on gear, including plastic boots necessary for the snow and ice climbing on Rainier, Hood, and Denali.

On our way from Spokane to the base camp the next morning, we rounded a corner in the road, and there it was – the awe-inspiring Mount Rainier.

Shafts of light illuminated the snow to a vibrant white, creating an intense contrast between it, the brilliant blue sky, and the giant green fir trees. At 14,411 feet high, the mountain's exquisite beauty took my breath away.

Mount Rainier, or Mount Tacoma as it is called by the local Native Americans, is classified as a dormant volcano. Dormant, not extinct.

Storms sweeping off the Pacific Ocean, as well as squalls produced on the mountain itself, make climbing hazardous at any time of the year.

Dr. George Draper, a famous psychologist, once said, "Man is at his worst when pitted against his fellow man. He is at his best when pitted against nature." By looking at the mountain's rugged majesty, I knew

Mount Rainier would demand my best.

Whit and I were the only members currently on our team. Rick had taken off as much time as he could and needed to get back to his family and work. Mike had to return to the Army base for a couple of weeks, but would be joining us again for Denali.

The remaining mountains leading up to Denali were Rainier, Hood, Boundary, and Whitney. Some of these were very technical mountains so it would be foolish climbing them with a two-man team. We'd be doing a great deal of roping up, and it is considerably safer to have three people roped together than two. Furthermore, neither Whit nor I had enough experience in crevasse rescue to be safe, and Rainier was riddled with crevasses.

At the lodge on Rainier's trailhead, I asked everyone I met if they could recommend a team we could join, or a solo climber who could join us. Lisa arranged for media coverage, so I did a couple of newspaper interviews in between my searches for a climber.

We needed to start our climb ASAP, and my stress increased as the hours passed and I still wasn't able to find anyone.

We spent the night at Whitaker's Bunkhouse and Coffee Shop. It was named after Lou Whittaker, a legend in the world of rock climbing. His brother, Jim, was actually the first American to summit Everest.

As we climbed out of the truck the following morning to begin our Rainier ascent, I prayed, "God, if it is your purpose for us to do this climb, send us someone to join our team. I want this climb to be safe." We couldn't delay any longer, so I had no choice but to proceed, holding tight to the faith it would work out.

We began our hike up Mount Rainier from Paradise Inn, a lodge at the base of the mountain. Skyline Trail, which leads from the lodge, had a number of day climbers on it who had no intention of going past the Muir Snowfields.

Several hours later we reached Muir Camp at 10,000 feet and made our way to the bunkhouse. Whit tossed his gear onto an open bunk. I rolled out my sleeping bag on a bunk nearby and took out my tape recorder to record the day's events. I was barely stretched out on the bag when a stranger burst through the door of the bunkhouse. "I understand there are two guys here who are looking for a climbing partner?"

I snapped alert. "That's us." I practically tripped over myself to meet him. "My name is Todd Huston."

"Hey! I'm Jim. Do you mind if I rope up with you?"

I was tempted, but needed to ask, "Have you done much climbing?"

The guy chuckled. "I guess you could say that. I've climbed in the Himalayas and the Alps."

"That's good enough for me." I grinned and shook his hand. "Welcome to the team." With a sense of relief and gratitude, I felt the stress melting away.

The exhaustion of the day was setting in and I realized how tired I felt. It was 9:00 p.m. and we all needed rest. I curled up in my sleeping bag and tried to sleep, but it was impossible with climbers constantly coming in and out of the bunkhouse. Finally Whit, Jim, and I decided our efforts to sleep were pointless, so headed back onto the mountain.

We left the lodge around midnight behind another climbing team. The moon was full and reflected off the snow so brightly we didn't need our headlamps on the glacial parts of the climb.

After crossing Cowlitz Glacier and the loose rocks of Cathedral Rocks, we walked up Ingraham Glacier, which is a field of snow and ice edged on both sides by major crevasses. We stopped to rest at the base of a massive ice wall.

A climber was talking about a tragic event that once occurred right in this location. "This is the place where a chunk of glacier broke apart, falling onto, and killing, a number of high school climbers."

I looked up at the wall of broken ice, which actually did seem ready to tumble down on us at any moment.

We traversed across the glacier to the base of Disappointment Cleaver and onto a steep trail with loose gravel. We scraped along in the dark with our ice axes and crampons, trying to follow a makeshift path through the cracks in the rocks.

Finally the sun started to rise. As we climbed, we watched the dark sky awaken into radiant hues of yellows, reds, and light pinks. Moments like this filled my soul with an amazing sense of peace and joy.

I continued up the long, steep path leading to the crater at the top, stopping periodically to catch my breath and kick balls of packed snow caught in my crampons.

At long last, after two days of continual climbing with only a few hours of sleep, we crossed the snow-filled crater to the summit – Columbia Point.

A sixty-mile-per-hour wind whipped around us, forcing us to put on extra gear to stay warm. Our eyes were watering and burning from the cold air. We located the outcropping of three rocks signifying the official summit and registered our climb.

We snapped the usual pictures, with Mount Adams and Mount St. Helens in the background. I also spotted Oregon's Mount Hood, which would be our next destination. I silently hoped it wouldn't be as difficult as this climb.

The way back down the mountain brought some unexpected surprises. With the sun now overhead we could clearly see dangers we hadn't known existed in the darkness of the night. Especially at Disappointment Cleaver and Cathedral Rocks. These were very narrow trails with severe drop-offs along the side of the mountain. One misstep would very likely have been fatal. In the middle of the night we were completely focused on the two to three feet illumined by our headlamps and had no idea of the potential risks.

We came to a snow bridge and decided we would belay across to be safe. Snow bridges frozen only hours ago had become soft and dangerous with the midday sun. We tested each step with our ice axes, searching for soft spots that might be hiding the blue-green crevasses. I peered down a number of them trying to see the bottom. It was eerie to think about climbers who had lost their lives by falling into these icy graves.

When we reached a smooth, gradual slope, I dropped onto my bottom.

"Let's glissade," I exclaimed to Whit and Jim.

Using my ice-axe to guide me, I slid several hundred yards down the snowfield like a kid on a toboggan. It gave my legs and lungs a much needed rest, and it was a lot of fun.

Toward the end of the descent, I met climbers who heard about me on the radio, in the newspapers, and on television. I also met a teenage boy who seemed to lack the motivation to learn. He didn't want to work for his grades, or participate in school activities.

As we walked, I told him about the adventure of climbing and what it meant to me.

"Find something you love and are passionate about," I told him.

I shared with him that he, like everyone, has a purpose and calling in life, and when he finds it, it will becomes his own unique way of reaching out and helping the world.

"Make that your goal," I urged him, "because then your education will be about more than just making good grades. It will be about learning how to learn, so you can progress faster toward your goals. That's when you'll find you have this inner drive to continually learn and grow. And it will propel you to the point where you have this desire to, not only help others, but teach them how to do it themselves, so they too can be a part of helping the world be a better place."

Following me into the lodge, he asked me more questions about my life. It was good to know I reached him, even if only in a small way.

I went in search of a pay phone to call Lisa.

"How are you doing at finding a guide for Mount Hood?" I asked. In the pit of my stomach, I had an eerie feeling Hood was going to be more of an adventure than I previously imagined.

"No luck so far. I've called every guide service in the Portland Yellow Pages, and no one is going up the mountain this week."

I rubbed my eyes with my hand. "We're so close to breaking the record. Hood is number forty-six. There must be someone."

I knew climbing Hood without a third party would be foolish. Like on Rainier, Whit and I lacked adequate experience on rescue techniques.

I called the headquarters of a recommended guide company and talked with the owner. I told him about our goal to break the current highpoint record, then reviewed with him the route we wished to follow. His answer left my heart in my stomach.

"If you climb that mountain with only two on your team, buddy, it's a death ride."

CHAPTER FOURTEEN

Held Hostage by Mount Hood

The danger on Mount Hood was not the cold, but the heat. An unexpected heat wave melted the snow at the summit exposing dirt and rock. During the colder part of the day, the ice held the rocks to the mountains. But when the unseasonably warmer temperatures increased, the ice melted and the rocks cut loose, tumbling down the mountain.

I called Lisa to tell her the grim news. "They say it's too dangerous."

"I'll keep trying," she assured me. "If you haven't found someone by the time I get to Portland, I'll help you make calls when I arrive. I'm sure there's an experienced guide willing to climb with you two."

Lisa planned to stay with her brother while we climbed Mount Hood and we'd connect afterward. It would be the last time we'd see each other before flying to Hawaii.

"Ready to roll?" Whit tapped me on the shoulder.

I nodded, wished Lisa a safe flight, and followed Whit out to the truck.

"Find a guide?" he asked as I climbed into the passenger seat.

"Not yet," There was no need to hide my disappointment – we were both concerned.

My foot ached, my stump ached, my back ached, and my head ached. Driving to Portland to face another problem was the last thing I wanted to do.

Whit glanced over at me as he eased the truck onto the highway. "What will we do if we can't find a guide?"

We'd both heard of the accident on Hood a week earlier. A team of five climbers fell. Two were killed, and two others were severely injured.

I leaned my head against the backrest and closed my eyes. "I don't know. Every one of the guide services recommends we stay off the mountain."

"That's easy for them to say," Whit mumbled. "They don't have a record to break."

Weary beyond words, I sighed. "I understand where they're coming from. They have their liability insurance and safety reputation on the line."

Exhaustion from the climb and stress of our situation lulled me into a semiconscious rest. When we hit the outskirts of Portland we headed straight for a hotel.

Whit staggered down the hallway ahead of me. Upon reaching his door, he waved his hand in the air. "See you next week."

I would have laughed at his joke if I had the energy to.

Once inside my room, I puttered about, finally working up the energy to take a shower and call my parents. I thought about Lisa flying into Portland and her brother being there to meet her. The more I thought about her, the more I knew I should be there too. I knew she'd love the surprise.

I flopped onto the bed, stared up at the ceiling, and yawned.

"But I'm too tired." I closed my eyes.

Suddenly my eyes flew open. "Face it Todd," I said to myself, "You want to go to the airport more than you want to sleep!"

I threw on my T-shirt, shorts, and shoe, rolled the sleeve over my stump holding my prosthesis, ran my fingers through my hair, and headed out the door.

Her brother recognized me from the news clipping she mailed him. We talked while we waited for the plane to arrive. I eagerly moved closer to the cordoned area and watched until she exited the jetway.

"Todd! I didn't expect to see you here!" she squealed, throwing her arms around my neck. I gave her a long hug. So much had happened since the last time I saw her. We discussed our guide problem all the way to the car.

She had good news. "I found a guide service that will take you up the mountain."

Like on Rainier, I felt the apprehension melt away, and said a silent, "Thank you," to God.

The next day she and Whit went sightseeing in Portland while I talked with the guide service. Eight hours before we were scheduled to do the climb, I got a message from them.

"No," I shouted. "You can't back out now!" But they did. I couldn't believe it. I had little choice but to resume my search.

I called another guide service. "No way, man." They wouldn't even listen to my plans. Next I called a man Whit met on Rainier who agreed to climb with us.

"Sorry. I can't do it," he said, apologetically.

"But you said…" I was ready to beg.

"That was before I heard the updates on the condition of the mountain. There are rocks the size of refrigerators tumbling down those slopes." He paused, probably waiting for my reply, but I was speechless. He continued, "The snow bridge is gone. We'd have less than a fifty-fifty chance of coming out alive."

I closed my eyes and rubbed the back of my neck. I'd heard it all before.

My head pounded from the tension knots in my neck. "What if we do an alternate route?"

"You'd be in even bigger trouble. Why don't you come back in a week?" he suggested.

"I can't do that," I told him. "Besides, it's only July. The longer we wait, the more the snow will melt and the worse the mountain will get."

I hung up the receiver. I began to wonder if everyone was right. Maybe I shouldn't try to go up there now. Was I just being bull-headed?

The thought occurred to call Fred. He might have a solution.

Fred had climbed Mount Elbrus in Russia, Kilimanjaro in Africa, and Aconcagua in South America and, most importantly, Mount Hood.

The phone rang three times before I heard Kathy's voice. "Fred and I cannot come to the phone right now, but if at the beep, you'll leave your message . . ."

"Auggh!!" I groaned. "Where are you?" I left a message, explaining the situation.

That evening Fred called. "Todd, I think the mountain can be climbed. You've come too far to quit now. If you'll pay the plane fare, I'll get off work and take you up."

The next morning at 9:30 I met Fred at the airport. He threw his bag into the truck.

"Let's go climb a mountain." I smiled.

I drove him to the hotel where we talked to Whit and Lisa about the climb.

"What if it's dangerous?" Lisa asked.

Fred shrugged. "If there's a problem, we'll find a way around it. We won't climb if it's not safe. I promise."

I felt comfortable with Fred's expertise and common sense. He'd recognize a dangerous situation and devise an alternate plan if necessary.

Considering the circumstances, the possibility of failure continued to loom in my thought. I knew for my message to have an impact I needed to finish this expedition and break the record. Going out there and saying, "I gave it my best shot," would fall way short.

"OK, God," I thought, "I'm putting this in your hands."

We piled into the truck and headed east across Morrison Bridge. Mount Hood floated above Portland like a fantasy mountain. It almost seemed unattainable and aloof.

We ate at Timberline Lodge and talked to the park rangers about the hazards.

The soft crunch of snow under my plastic boot settled into a comfortable rhythm as I followed Fred up the base of the mountain. The warmer temperatures of the early evening allowed us to do the lower part of the mountain in hiking shorts and long-sleeved shirts. Later on, as we reached higher altitudes, we'd have to add layers of heavy clothing.

We hiked off the pathway and onto the trail. Lisa ran ahead of us, then dropped behind us, snapping photos of Whit, Fred, and me as we climbed. When the trail grew tougher she returned to the lodge while Whit, Fred, and I continued up the mountain.

"Come on." Fred waved his arm. "Let's do this!"

I tested my weight in the snow beside the trail. "The snow is good and solid."

Whit kicked at a clump of snow with the toe of his hiking boot. "Feels OK to me."

Satisfied, Fred turned and headed up the ski slope.

Trekking up the hill beyond the ski area, my boot and the foot of my artificial limb kept sinking into the soft ground, sliding back a half step with each step forward. Fred adjusted his pace accordingly.

We hiked past the second lodge without stopping, but a mile farther couldn't help but pause to watch the amazing sunset. The colors faded against the hills to the west of Portland. One after another, the lights blink on until they were like little diamond chips scattered across a stretch of dark, velvety blue.

That's when the temperature dropped dramatically, forcing us into heavier clothing.

Before starting out again we talked over our game plan. We decided to camp at Hogback Ridge, directly below the summit, sleep from midnight until 4:00 a.m., the absolute coldest hour of the night, then charge to the summit and back down again before it got too warm.

"If we get to our campsite fast enough, I'll help you guys set up and scout the mountain to find out what's happening," Fred suggested.

The crisp night air stung my cheeks and invigorated my step as we hiked across rock-strewn ridges. Using our ice axes, but not our crampons, we crossed a field of snow and ice. I took each step with caution. If I slipped, I'd be taking a long sleigh ride down.

We came to the base of a treacherous slope of solid ice, the last measure of ice before cresting Hogback Ridge. The only light was from our headlamps.

Fred pointed toward the top of the ridge. "There it is. Let's go on up."

Looking at the slick surface of the walls and comparing them to the slope I had just climbed, I pulled my crampons out of my pack. "Looks a little icy. I'm going to put these on first."

"Awe Todd! It's not that bad," Fred teased. "But you go ahead, I'm moving forward."

He did too. All of five feet. Then, struggling to catch his footing, he spun out like a small car trying to accelerate on an icy hill. When he regained his footing, he inched back down the wall in a controlled slide.

He slid to a stop and grinned. "I think I'll put my crampons on now." Whit and I laughed.

We slowly inched up the slope to the top of the two hundred-foot ridge. All conversation and banter ceased. Each step required total concentration.

One wrong move and we'd be rolling down to the gnarled outcroppings on the lower part of the mountain. Looking down you could make out the massive piano-sized rocks that had tumbled from the cliff and dotted the ice field a thousand yards below.

We hacked our way up, and as we pulled ourselves over the top we were shocked at what we saw. The area where we'd be sleeping was only eighteen inches wide with steep slopes falling away at the side. We hiked around until we found a spot barely wide enough and made camp.

Removing our packs, we anchored them to the mountain. With our ice axes, we each carved out individual campsites, just large enough to spread out one sleeping bag. Next, we piled snow along the downhill edge of our bags, which would hopefully prevent us from rolling down the side of the mountain in our sleep.

Once satisfied with our fortresses, we pounded our axes into the snow and tied our sleeping bags to them. With any luck, if the make-shift snow wall didn't hold, the axes would keep us from sliding down the three hundred-foot slope.

"Sweet dreams, Todd," I joked with myself.

CHAPTER FIFTEEN

Whitney – Number Forty-Eight

"Phew!" Whit straightened up and wrinkled his nose. "What stinks?"

Fred laughed. "That's the sulfur fumes."

Mount Hood is an active volcano, so gas works its way up from the magma chamber deep inside of it and comes out through vents, tainting the air with a rancid egg smell.

We ate handfuls of trail mix and fell asleep watching the tendrils of sulfur fumes rising from of the side of the mountain.

When 4:00 a.m. arrived I was shivering in the sub-freezing temperatures. A cold front had moved in while we slept, bringing even lower temperatures than we hoped for, thank God. We packed the barest essentials in our summit packs before taking off.

I put on my helmet, strapped into my climbing harness, roped up, and started up the ridge. I glanced down and spotted some other climbers behind us. They stopped when they saw us so they wouldn't be at risk from falling rocks we might inadvertently send rolling down the slope.

We came to a bergschrund, similar to the one on Rainier, which stopped us in our tracks.

A narrow tongue of snow stretched across the chasm. It was the snow bridge guides and rangers said no longer existed. Whit and I braced ourselves as Fred tested its strength.

"It's OK," he called back, shifting his feet across the open crevasse. Upon reaching the other side and securing his ice axe into the mountain, he signaled for me to cross.

I held my breath and inched across the bridge of snow and ice, certain at any moment I'd break through and find myself swinging a thousand or more feet above the abyss below like a spider on a thread. I let out a long breath when I reached the other side. Whit came safely across behind me.

Our next challenge was a slushy area of loose rock, dirt, and ice. Normally snow covered these rocks, but due to the warm temperatures they were now exposed. My crampons refused to dig into the mottled surface. Every step dislodged rocks, sending them tumbling down the mountain. Fred crossed and waited on the other side, while Whit followed behind.

The slope grew steeper. The rocks close to the top were much larger, and we crawled slowly over them. Suddenly, my foot broke one of them loose from the mountain, sending it crashing to the valley below. I dug my crampon into a crag in a nearby rock.

"This is getting nasty," I exclaimed.

We passed the crux of the mountain, crawling up a gully of mud, snow, ice, and loose rock. My hands and clothing coated in mud, I scrambled to the ridge in time to see the sun rise over the mountain ranges to the east.

Fred rushed ahead to the summit, turned, and shouted, "We made it!"

Whit and I rushed to the top, high-fived one another, and signed the register.

"Time for some quick pictures." Fred put his camera on a rock, set the automatic timer, and ran to Whit and me. The camera clicked. We repeated the process with each other's cameras.

Even though we needed to hurry off the summit, I paused. My gaze swept the horizon. I was standing on the back of a gargantuan, restless, smoke-belching monster. To the east I saw a succession of mountain ranges flattening out into a high chaparral. To the south was Mount Jefferson, named by Lewis and Clark after the president who funded their exploration, and the Three Sisters, three volcanic peaks standing watch over the town of Bend. I turned toward the north where I saw the famous Columbia Gorge, which challenged the pioneers who headed west. To the west the lights of Portland blinked off for another day.

"Todd." I felt Fred's hand on my shoulder. "I'm glad you asked me to do this climb with you."

I smiled. "Me too. You don't know how important you've been to the entire expedition. Getting us up a mountain no one else was willing to . . ."

"Yes," he interrupted, "but you're the one who's gone the distance. This climb is yours, remember?"

Silently we stood side by side for several minutes, watching the morning roll in on the valleys below – two lifelong friends sharing our moment of triumph.

Fred picked up his pack. "We've got to get out of here."

Reluctantly I tightened the strap on my helmet and prepared to leave. It was the same feeling on every difficult summit – so much work and so little time to enjoy the accomplishment.

I would have loved to stay on the mountain longer, to study the ever-changing moods of the terrain. I wondered what it would be like to lie under the canopy of stars, or watch the moon rise, from the perspective of the summit. The mountain seemed permanent, unshakable. I felt the presence of an unseen Power.

But I also felt cold, was in a hostile environment, and wanted to get down.

Once we started back I remembered my concern about the climb down. The route was more dangerous since the sun was up. We watched each other carefully as we started down the trail, leaving only our faint footprints and signatures in the register as proof of our presence on the mountain.

While it was very slippery, the descent itself was much easier than I expected. I stopped to take off my crampons when we reached the rocks. Whit stayed with me while Fred ran ahead to begin packing the gear. He had a plane to catch in Portland so we were short on time.

"Todd, can you be down by nine?" Fred asked.

"I'll give it my best shot," I promised.

Fred waved and ran down the mountain.

A few minutes later Whit and I got back on the trail. When we reached the ski slope area, I laid down on my back and glissaded down the mountain, while Whit followed Fred's lead and ran.

Finding a safe area, I glissaded past skiers and snow boarders. After passing the smaller lodge, I glissaded a bit more, then took off running.

Throwing my head back to the wind, I picked up speed. Suddenly, without any warning, my artificial leg blew out beneath me, sending me sprawling into the snow.

Somehow, it didn't even hurt. I checked it out to see what happened and saw the clip holding the spring in my leg had popped off. I pawed through my pack until I found a spare, then started running down the trail again. I made it to Timberline Lodge only twenty minutes behind Fred, who was with Lisa watching for us. Whit arrived right behind me.

After tossing our gear in the truck we loaded into the cab and headed for Portland International Airport. If we didn't hurry Fred would miss his flight. Whit took the challenge to heart, and after a wild trip, with tires squealing on some sharp curves, he pulled the truck to a stop in front of the departing gate five minutes before takeoff.

Fred leaped out of the truck and began to grab his gear.

"Leave it," I shouted. "We'll bring it to Reno tomorrow."

Fred nodded and dashed into the terminal. Lisa and I followed behind in case he missed his flight. At the gate I asked the attendant if he made it.

She nodded. "The door to the jetway was already closed, but we opened it for him."

"Nothing like a close call to add a little excitement to the trip," I smiled at Lisa.

We dropped Lisa off at her brother's house so she could fly back to California to finalize the Hawaii plans. Whit and I hopped on the I-5 which heads south through California. Though we were more than five hundred miles away from home, we cheered when we crossed the Oregon-California border. We experienced the same exhilaration when we crossed into the Pacific Time Zone earlier in the trip. We crossed time zone lines numerous times so far.

We then headed east to Nevada and stayed with Fred and Kathy in Reno that night, afterward driving south to Boundary Peak, Nevada's 13,140-foot high point, the next day.

Located down a desolate road on the California-Nevada border, the desert peak is considered to be a strenuous climb. For me, the most strenuous part of the climb was having no source of drinking water along the 7.4-mile trail.

Once we were at the peak, we relaxed, enjoying the scenery. We looked west toward the horizon trying to guess which peak was Mount Whitney, our next high point.

I returned on the same trail we climbed up, but Whit chose to go back by a different trail he saw from the summit.

As I walked through a wide valley I heard a horse neighing. I whipped about in time to see a pack of wild Mustangs. Nearby, a young colt stood close to its mother's side. Suddenly the mare saw me and protectively reared up on her hind legs.

"Hey, guys." I backed slowly away. "It's OK."

I ducked behind a bush off to one side, then skirted around the area. The mustangs, too, moved cautiously in the other direction, both of us hedging around one another.

Whit was asleep in the front seat by the time I reached the truck. After I drank what seemed like a gallon of water, I tossed my gear into the back of the truck and climbed aboard. We headed toward California's John Muir Wilderness and Mount Whitney.

Whit arranged to meet David Long, one of his buddies, at a motel in the town of Lone Pine. David wanted to hike the last mountain in the continental U.S. with us.

Climbers can camp overnight on Whitney's summit, but doing so requires a permit. They are issued daily at the ranger's station by lottery, and the earlier you get there the better. We turned in close to 9:00 that night so we could wake up early.

The next morning Whit got up at the crack of dawn and drove to the ranger's station. It would really throw a wrench in our plans if it didn't work out. Fortunately, we got the luck of the draw and were on the trail by eleven. We projected an eight-and-a-half-hour trek, four hours to the trail camp, a half-hour to rest, then four hours to the summit.

Whit and his friend started out ahead of me from Whitney Portal, where we left the truck. Muscles hardened by a summer of climbing, and spirits pumped to complete all fifty high points, I moved with speed and agility up the trail. Whenever I passed other climbers, I stopped and talked, then sped up to resume my climb. I felt like a well-tuned machine as I hiked over streams and past lakes with ease. How different this climb was from my earlier mountain experiences!

At the Outpost Camp I met a really sweet girl who was a recent high school graduate. She and her mother were climbing the mountain together. After hearing my story the girl admitted to her fears of beginning college in the fall. She and her mom were obviously close, and I could tell she was raised in a very tight-knit family. I talked with her about some of the ideas I had shared with the family in Florida whose children were getting ready to start a new school. However there was something else exciting about her upcoming life-adventure I wanted her to think about.

"Not everyone has the great fortune of growing up in the type of loving, happy family environment you did," I shared with her. "You have the opportunity to radiate love and joy with everyone you encounter, and it'll be a gift that will help them grow within their own lives. And because you obviously approach your life expecting good, some amazing opportunities will come your way! You will make some special lifelong friends, and likely find career path you become excited to pursue."

Her smile grew broader with every idea we discussed and she admitted to feeling much better about it. She, her mother, and I said a friendly good-bye and returned to our hiking.

I knew the challenge of Mount Whitney was the switchbacks. Whit counted ninety-seven winding up the hillside. I dreaded them from the moment I first heard of them from other climbers. To my surprise, they made the climb much easier.

"Just goes to show," I thought, "how crazy it is to go into something with the expectancy of bad. It's just a matter of perspective."

Mount Whitney is 14,495 feet of granite. The highest mountain in the lower forty-eight, it is the result of the Sierra-Nevada fault system. Over the last two to ten million years the granite has been pushed up from below the surface. Walls of it edge the well-marked trail. As you look toward the summit, you can see granite spires, like fingers, reaching into the sky, competing with each other for the coveted position of highest point in California. Without the trail markers it would be difficult to tell which pinnacle to climb. It's easy to see how Clarence King, a member of a survey team in the mid-1800's, made two attempts to summit, and both times climbed the wrong peak. He was hoping to be the first to accomplish this feat, however due to his mistakes, two other climbers beat him to it.

I caught up to Whit and David at the 12,000-foot Trail Camp. We stopped to pump water from the lake with our purifiers before continuing.

Due to the high altitudes we had already climbed, Whit and I weren't feeling the effect of the altitude here. David, however, showed signs of fatigue in his movements and face. Concerned, I handed him half of a tablet a doctor had given me for altitude sickness.

"Keep it handy just in case we get separated or something," I advised.

We resumed our climb to the summit. The sun was going down as we reached the ridge leading to the high point. From the ridge, I could see clear to the town of Lone Pine and across the desolate high plains of eastern Nevada.

The sound of a helicopter landing on top of the mountain averted my attention and gave me a surreal feeling. It reminded me of the ending of the movie *K2* Fred and I watched months ago. As the chopper flew quickly away I knew a climber was in trouble. I hoped everything was OK.

As we hiked on, we spotted the small stone hut at the summit built by the Smithsonian Institute in 1909 as a protection from lightning.

"Yes!" Despite the fact I had been hiking for eight hours I broke into a run. Adrenaline pumped through my body as I charged up the last few yards to the summit. I threw my hands into the air. "We made it!"

An orange glow filled the sky, and I felt buoyant with joy. Another challenge met, another victory gained. Barring an unforeseen accident, I knew we were on our way to the big one.

After registering and snapping pictures of each other, we headed toward the sleeping hut. I asked a climber nearby about the helicopter.

"Some guy got a bad case of elevation sickness and had to be flown to the hospital." At least they were able to fly him out to take care of him.

I took my cell phone out of my backpack after dinner and dialed Fred's number in Reno.

"Hey, Kathy! Fred there?"

Several seconds passed before I heard my friend's voice.

"I'm calling you from the summit of Whitney – we made it!"

"Incredible!" Fred laughed.

134

"So we'll be headed to Alaska Saturday morning. Can you believe it? We actually made it this far, and are headed to Alaska!"

True to his sarcastic nature, Fred stated, "I wish I could join you, but I have a real job."

CHAPTER SIXTEEN

Heading to Alaska

We drove south from Mount Whitney toward Los Angeles to catch our flight to Alaska. I was excited. And extremely nervous.

As we drove over the mountains into the L.A. basin, I saw one of the worst sights I had ever seen.

"This is absolutely disgusting," I told Whit.

The brown smog settling into the valleys was like sludge. After spending so much time amongst the beauty of mountains, prairies, deserts, and woodlands, I was shocked by the ugliness of pollution. The magnificent natural beauty of the mountains skirting L.A. was veiled by a dirty, brown haze.

Whit was too caught up in the anticipation of our upcoming climb to hear what I was saying. He glanced over at me from the driver's seat, his eyes bright with excitement.

"Can you believe it, man? We're heading for the big one! Denali!" He pounded his hand on the steering wheel.

Everything I heard about the killer mountain reinforced my fears. Books, pamphlets, magazine articles, and experienced climbers warned of the genuine dangers inherent in a Denali assault – the crevasses, the glaciers, the sheer ice walls, the violent storms, plummeting temperatures, whiteouts. Leaning my head back against the headrest, I closed my eyes. A vision passed before me – a vision of walking across the snow, hearing a loud crack, and disappearing into a crevasse, frozen and lost forever. The same video had played in my mind for weeks.

Caught in a maze of nagging self-doubt and fear, I continued to brood over the potential tragedies Denali promised. Thoughts of dying on that mountain refused to be silenced. I seemed to be hypnotized by the negativity.

"No!" I proclaimed, as if to wake myself up. "I have not been led on this journey to die. God does not operate like that. He's a God of love and good, not fear and evil. He inspired this mission and created me with everything necessary to accomplish it."

Though these thoughts brought me a great deal of comfort, a twinge of fear lingered. Denali loomed like a gigantic obstacle between me and my ability to get my message out to the world.

The next morning we boarded the plane for Seattle. Eager to be underway, Whit bounded ahead of me down the jetway. A blend of excitement and dread stirred within me as I located my seat and prepared for takeoff.

Then I smiled to myself as something Fred once said to me came to mind. "Let the fear go and simply enjoy the ride, Todd!"

Enjoying myself was a new thought. I worked so long and hard preparing for this moment there had been little time to actually enjoy myself. I mulled over the strange concept throughout the flight.

The jet flew over the California coastline toward Canada. Though I stared out the window for the entire flight, I couldn't remember anything I saw, because all I could think about was Denali.

I'd been shown numerous times throughout my life the incredible power within that could get me through anything. I knew power didn't come from me, but God, so it was something everyone had. I realized demonstrating this was the whole point of my life journey, and conquering this monster of a mountain would give me the voice I needed to share this message with the world. If a one-legged amputee could scale massive ice walls and stand victorious on top of the North American continent, so could thousands of other people take hope and triumph over impossible odds in their lives.

A knot formed in my throat. I swallowed hard. "OK, God. It's you and me – from the first to the last."

We changed planes in Seattle. Though it was 2:00 a.m. by the time we landed in Anchorage, the lingering sunlight made it appear as though it was hours earlier.

The next morning I called Lisa. She said, "You really need video footage of your climb, Todd. The TV stations I've contacted are asking for it. And later, when you go out to speak, you'll wish you had it." I could imagine her tapping her number-two pencil on the desktop in my guest bedroom, the base of operations for *Summit America*.

"I know. I promise I'll see what I can do," I replied.

I called Adrian Crane when we arrived, our guide for the Denali ascent. His British accent and droll wit came through the phone lines. "All's A-OK on my end," he assured me. "Mike is with me and we'll see you tomorrow."

I met Adrian several months ago at a *50 Peaks Project* meeting. He was the highpoint record holder, and was hired to guide the group up Denali. When the project dissolved, I asked him to guide the *Summit America* team, and he accepted.

The next morning we hired a taxi, a yellow Subaru station wagon from Denali Overland Transportation, and headed for the REI store. Mike looked like a kid in a candy store as we purchased the necessary snow tents, additional rope, snowshoes, sleeping bags, camping gear, and extra batteries. We also rented the plastic boots and gaiters necessary for snow climbing. I eyed the growing mound of gear.

"Is that all?" the clerk asked. I gulped and nodded.

He didn't even blink when he tabulated the bill. "That will be $3,115, Mr. Huston, after your twenty percent discount, of course."

Though I knew our safety depended on using the right gear, I reluctantly removed my checkbook from my jacket pocket.

As we loaded the gear into the taxi, I noted the physical contrasts between my three team members upon whom I was entrusting my life.

First there was Whit, the 6'2" outgoing and muscular guy who could always turn a pretty woman's head.

Then there was the wiry Englishman with the easy smile, Adrian. Though small, he was extremely strong and had the experience to do this climb. His eyes revealed the serious undertones and competitive spirit beneath his outgoing, laid-back attitude. Growing up in the mountains of Scotland gave him an incredible sixth sense for mountain weather.

And of course, Mike. He embodied a seriousness and determination that spoke of experience and confidence. Years of military training contributed to his detailed planning skills. His massive forearms bore witness to his years of rock climbing. We called him Popeye.

As Whit hurled the last package into the rear of the car, he straightened and looked around. "Hey, I'm hungry! When do we eat?"

I laughed. Whit was always hungry. We had just eaten before our shopping spree in REI. The humor of the situation gave me a sense that everything was normal and right with the world.

Let it go and enjoy the ride, Todd, I reminded myself.

After another quick bite, we headed for Talkeetna.

That night in the bunkhouse I listened to other climbers telling about their harrowing experiences on the mountain: their mistakes, what they would do differently, and what they would never do again. I also heard stories of climbers who didn't make it.

"One couple, a gung-ho army guy and his girlfriend, learned the hard way a few days back," one of the climbers volunteered. "They hiked to the summit from the 14,200-foot base camp instead of 17,200. On their way back down, on Denali Pass, the guy slipped and fell. In an attempt to stop his fall, he grabbed his girlfriend and ended up taking her with him."

I listened in horror as he continued, "They rolled more than five hundred feet down the slope and lacked the strength to climb out. That's where other climbers found them. By the time the rescue team got to the scene, the woman was dead – not from the fall, but from exposure. Her boyfriend lived, but lost some toes and fingers as well as part of his feet."

Another guy piped in, "People push themselves beyond their abilities all of the time. This year on Mount Washington a climber pushed himself and his friend too hard and they ended up falling. He survived, but his friend didn't."

I shuddered at the images of death the stories conjured up in my mind. I recalled the many times my mother cautioned me to learn from other people's mistakes. Words of wisdom, for sure.

Was I really ready for Denali? Tomorrow I would find out – one way or the other.

CHAPTER SEVENTEEN

Through Kahiltna Pass

Life at the Kahiltna Glacier was busy with the bustle of last minute preparations for the climb.

"Hello there. How's everything going?" It was Peter, one of the two climbers from the camp next to ours.

We invited him and his climbing partner, Chuck, to join us. They were both in their fifties, experienced climbers, and called themselves the Peter Pan Expedition Team. "You know, after the fairy-tale character who refused to grow up. Chuck and I are following his example." We all laughed.

I learned Peter was an emergency room physician. It made me feel better there was a medical doctor on the mountain. Then I remembered the people who were trapped under layers of ice for twenty or more years. A doctor wouldn't help much in that situation.

We spent all day transporting our gear to the 7,500-foot camp, which gave me plenty of time to wax poetic about Denali. Old Denali is wild, unpredictable, and tangled. Her cliffs of rock soar thousands of feet straight into the sky, glaciers apron her snowcapped peaks, and the roar of an avalanche echoes through her valleys. She is magnificent, dangerous, and beautiful all at the same time.

The next morning as we loaded our packs, I pushed any negative thoughts from my mind and gave in to the thrill of the climb.

We roped up. First our guide, Mike, then Whit, me, and Adrian. It was important to place the two experienced climbers on each end so if one fell into a crevasse the other could rescue them.

We trekked out to the main part of the glacier following previous climbers' tracks in the snow and headed north toward the glowering giant. I glanced back hoping to catch one last glimpse of the camp, but it was already swallowed up in the mist. Only a sea of gray met my gaze.

The hike up Ski Hill seemed to go on forever, especially considering we were all carrying sixty-five pound packs and pulling thirty pound sleds. The packs carried our personal items, like clothing, while the sleds held basic gear, such as food, ropes, and tents.

Furthermore, the altitude made every breath a struggle, and each step on my prosthesis sent a sharp pain up my stump.

It takes an amputee thirty percent more energy to walk than it does a two-legged person. In addition there are sores, swelling, rashes, and blisters caused by the artificial limb to contend with. One infected blister could prevent the success of the entire expedition because it feels like sandpaper across raw flesh.

We stopped for the night at the 9,500-foot camp. While Whit repaired the snow walls around our campsite, Adrian and I shoveled the area clear of the drifting snow until we had a smooth, level floor for our tents. In the meantime, Mike carved out a protected spot for our stove. Before long he had a kettle of snow melted for hot chocolate. I felt the same thrill creating our campsite I used to get building snow forts when I was a kid.

The next step in setting up the camp was carving out a restroom. Throughout all of my reading in preparation for the hike, I never thought about this very necessary facility. A mountain restroom consists of a seating area with a hole in the middle and a disposable plastic bag arranged beneath the hole. After use, the plastic bag is replaced by another. To dispose of the used bag, the team must rope up, walk to the edge of a deep crevasse, and toss the bag into it. Usually the bag disappears from sight, never to be seen again. If not, it must be retrieved and thrown again.

On one excursion, Mike needed to walk farther out onto the glacier than normal to throw the bag out of sight. We roped up with him in case he had any difficulties. On his trip back we heard a loud pop and the ground beneath us shifted downward a few inches. Mike quickly leaped to safety, afraid the ice beneath his feet would give way and send him plummeting into a crevasse.

Though crevasses pose one of the gravest dangers on the mountain, they are breathtakingly beautiful – deep blue-green ice twisting and curving endlessly downward skirted by pristine white snow. It seemed a shame to pollute them, especially with man-made plastic that would still be around for thousands of years. But realistically there was no other option in this land of snow and ice.

The next day I stayed behind at 9,500 while Mike, Whit, and Adrian took our gear up to the camp at 11,200 feet. Even though my legs weren't injured or overtired, I had to take extra care to keep my stump strong.

After my team dropped our gear off at 11,200 they came back to 9,500 to sleep.

There is less oxygen at higher elevations, which makes it harder for people to breathe and can cause altitude sickness. In the most extreme cases it causes Acute Mountain Sickness (AMS) which can be fatal. Therefore, it is crucial for individuals to give their body's time to acclimate when climbing to a higher elevation than they are accustomed to.

One way climbers acclimatize is to "climb high and sleep low." They carry their gear up to the next camp and come back down to sleep. Though staying at 9,500 feet while my team went to 11,200 was necessary for my stump, and it was nice to have a day during which my body could rest, I was concerned I wasn't acclimatizing.

The next day we hiked up to the 11,200-foot camp, which is at the base of Motorcycle Hill. While my team carried our gear up to 14,200, I cleared out a snow cave started by climbers earlier in the season. It was a great place to store our gear and would give us shelter if a major storm came through.

When Whit, Mike, and Adrian made it back down to 11,200, we sat inside one of our tents discussing our climbing plans for next couple of days.

While eating some crackers, peanut butter, and cheese, we spotted climbers coming down the mountain. Hunched against the wind with shoulders drooping, they plodded like robots toward the camp, every step a chore.

As they drew closer, I recognized the beard of Vern Tejas, a famous mountaineer and guide. I realized it was the team I'd almost booked to do this climb with a month ago, however, after praying about it, decided to stay with my own team.

"Hey," Adrian waved them over. "What happened? You guys look totally hammered."

"We are," one of the climbers replied, his face devoid of all animation, his eyes dulled by fatigue. "Got snowed in at the 17,200-foot camp for nine days. Lousy weather. Forty below and high winds. Miserable."

I thought about what these guys must have been through. Trapped in a tent with a limited supply of food, freezing temperatures, and no way to escape from the dangers if it got worse.

"Did you summit?" Mike asked.

Another rough looking climber, the energy beaten out of him, dropped his pack in the snow, "No. Couldn't. When we got our first break in the weather we high-tailed it for home." His voice attested to his intense disappointment. He began setting up his camp beside ours. "I don't know what happened to the other team who went out before us. Never did see them again."

"Other team?" Whit strolled over to join the conversation.

"Yeah, two Koreans. One's a park service employee and the other a trainee. They were just day climbing, off to the west of the primary route."

Mike took a sip from his mug. "Probably burrowed in on the mountain until the storm passed."

The climber frowned. "They weren't equipped for the cold weather."

Seeing the worried look on my face, Adrian added, "I'm sure they're fine."

I made my way over to Vern. "Sir, are you by any chance Vern Tejas?"

The man straightened and eyed me respectfully. A grin spread across his worn and tired face. "You're quite observant."

He glanced down at my exposed artificial leg. "And you're that young hiker who's out to break the highpoint record. Sit down. Let's talk."

I stretched my hand out to meet his. "It's such an honor to meet you, sir. I've read about you in all my hiking journals. You're a legend."

Among Vern's many climbing feats, he was the first to complete a winter solo on this mountain. It was incredible to think what it took to accomplish that.

The mountaineer studied my face for a moment. "And you, you're quickly becoming one. I can't tell you how much I admire you, taking on such a challenge as Denali with only one leg. You'll have quite a story to tell your grandchildren one day."

I smiled with pleasure. "I believe everybody who attempts to overcome a challenge has a story to tell. I mean, what you all have gone through these last nine days? You survived against some amazing odds and made it down safely. That was much more of a challenge than summiting on a bright, sunny day."

"You're probably right."

I was glad when one of the members of his climbing team offered to take our picture together. I knew I'd want to remember my encounter with this mountaineering great.

"I saw a tape of you on *Good Morning, America* a few days ago," I mentioned to him.

He grinned. "I suppose I'll be seeing you there in a few weeks."

I shrugged. "Maybe."

We talked about the current climb. I wished I had the courage to tell him of my fears. Somehow I thought he would have understood.

"No one is summiting right now," he said. "The windows in the storm aren't big enough to make it possible."

We both fell silent. Then he continued, "Be smart when climbing the Great One. She's unforgiving. One miscalculation and it's over. Take your time."

I stared at the snow melting around the base of the camp stove's flickering flame.

Didn't summit. The team didn't summit. And I could have been with them. If I had been, the entire highpoint project would have been scrapped. I couldn't have climbed the mountain a second time and broken the record. I had prayed for wisdom when deciding to go with Vern's team or mine. God seemed to be reassuring me once again of His leading.

CHAPTER EIGHTEEN

Death on the Mountain

It was time to rope up and head to our next camp at 14,200 feet. We said goodbye to our new friends, threw on our backpacks, and headed out.

The first hour-and-a-half took us up Motorcycle Hill. The bulge of snow above us looked as though it was ready to pop at any moment, and I was relieved when we made it through without an avalanche.

We spent the next six hours keeping a hyper vigilant watch for crevasses as we hiked across snow fields. We rounded Windy Corner, toe-to-toe, and gazed down into the emerald crevasse lining the glacier.

I marveled at the natural beauty of the mountain. I had crevasses below and avalanches above, and nowhere to escape if the mountain decided to unleash its sheer power. For the first time since I'd started the climb I began to feel the awesome strength of the Great One.

As I continued climbing, my breathing became more labored, and though it was bitterly cold I was sweating as though it was a hot, humid, Oklahoma summer day. I worried about dehydration so I made sure I took in more fluids than usual.

Once we rounded Windy Corner we ascended toward the 14,200 camp, which was alive with activity. It looked like a small city with people and tents everywhere. The wide expanse of snowy fields had glaciers at the edge, but the main camp area was solid ground. Climbers like it because they can roam around freely without fear of falling into a crevasse. Whatever isolation I felt earlier gave way to tents, radio antennae, laughter, the aroma of food cooking, and the comings and goings of a helicopter. I felt a complete sense of safety for the first time since starting my ascent on the mountain.

Though I felt great mentally, my stomach was another story. Before we began settling in for the night, it was rumbling and gurgling. The ache was so intense I could hardly put one foot in front of the other.

"I'm really tired. I think I may have altitude sickness," I told Whit.

He laughed and waved me away. "It's all in your head."

"I don't think so. We had a sharp rate of ascent today, and I feel nauseous, exhausted, and really weak."

Mike overhead what I said. "Todd, you'll be fine. It won't be a problem, I assure you."

Adrian added his assurances. "There's nothing to worry about. I've been up and down mountains all my life and never once gotten AMS. Besides, it's all in the head." He tapped his forehead.

"Tell that to my stomach." I looked at my unsympathetic climbing partners with frustration.

"I'm going over to the ranger tent," I said dryly.

The ranger tent seemed a lot further away than it actually was. The closer I got, the worse I felt. My thoughts flashed to the summit and I grew very concerned about my ability to continue. If I had a bad case of AMS the doctor would send me back down the mountain to be admitted into a hospital. It would be the end of my record-breaking attempt.

I stumbled into the ranger station and asked the ranger on duty, "How do I find out if I have altitude sickness?"

The man eyed me critically for a moment. "Come around to the medical tent. There's a simple test we can administer that will measure the amount of oxygen in your blood."

I followed him to the round tent where the medical supplies were kept.

"Got a possible AMS here for you, Doc," he called out.

The doctor, an emergency physician from Boulder, Colorado, gestured for me to sit on a white metal stool. "So you're feeling kind of punk, huh?"

I nodded, telling him all my symptoms.

"Have you ever been higher than 14,000 feet before?"

"A few times in the lower forty-eight," and added with a slight smile, "and then of course there were those pain killers I used to take."

He grinned. "You haven't lost your sense of humor, anyway. That's a good sign."

He clamped my finger to an instrument that flashed red digital numbers.

"Well, it says here you only have seventy-three percent of the required amount of oxygen in your blood. You have a mild case of altitude sickness."

My heart dropped to my feet as I began to feel anxious for my health and the success of the climb.

He continued, "The good news is, it's mild enough we won't need to take drastic measures. I'll give you some pills to increase your respiration, which, in turn, will pump more oxygen into your blood. But I'd advise only taking half a tablet because of the tingling in your fingers and frequent urination they can cause." He further advised, "And be sure you drink lots of fluids."

I thanked him and headed slowly back to my tent. I hoped the symptoms didn't get worse the higher I got on the mountain. Still, I experienced a grim satisfaction when I told my teammates my symptoms were real and not just in my head.

After drinking a cup of hot soup, I crawled into my sleeping bag, pulled the hood over my head, and slept the entire night. Often people have trouble sleeping at such high altitudes, but not me. I slept great that night. By the next morning my symptoms were completely gone and I felt much stronger.

Later that morning my team set off to make a carry up to 16,800 feet, where they stashed our cache in the snow.

While the three of them were gone I came across a younger climber named Rocky. He ambled over to our campsite to introduce himself.

Rocky was a Princeton graduate and trust fund kid who was living the life of a ski bum in Aspen, Colorado. He told me how he and Kelly, his climbing partner, had done pot while hiking on the mountain. He pushed his long, straggly hair away from his face. "Yeah, it was really cool, dude. A real trip."

"Weren't you afraid of not being able to think clearly in case there was an avalanche, or you came across crevasse?"

"Everything was cool. Besides we can handle the stuff."

"I hope so, for your sake." I knew all too well how the body can build a tolerance to drugs and then one day have a very bad reaction to it.

"So when do you plan to summit?" he asked.

"By the end of the week."

He nodded his head in agreement. "That's cool. Hey, dude, I got a couple of ounces. Do you want some?"

"Naw." I shook my head. "I don't use the stuff."

He studied the lighted joint perched between his thumb and middle finger. "Do you think this altitude could be really bad for me? I've been smoking dope all the way up the mountain."

I shrugged. "I'd quit if I were you."

He thought for a moment, waved an idle hand, and said, "Maybe I will."

I took a deep breath and filled my lungs with the cold, clean mountain air. I couldn't imagine taking drugs on a mountain climb. Besides the very real danger, it seemed like such a waste. Being in the outdoors is about health, fresh air, and feeling a oneness with nature and God.

When the team returned to camp, Whit was feeling quite sick. The Headwall had been rough on him. We discussed the possibility of waiting an extra day until he felt better.

"No, I'll be fine by morning," he announced.

The perpetual athlete, Whit was constantly pushing his endurance to its limits, possibly at a cost to him and the team. He had yet to learn the strength of youth doesn't always overcome adversity. However, I admired his never-quit attitude and willingness to help others with their heavy loads.

I had a kettle of hot soup bubbling on the stove ready for them. We clustered around our portable radio to hear Ranger Annie give the weather forecast while we ate.

"There is currently a low-pressure system on the mountain that looks like it will last for another day. There is a possibility of a high-pressure system moving in behind it."

While we knew the rangers' approach to forecasting weather was to keep people from taking unnecessary risks, we groaned at the news. Another day of bad weather at the summit. At least it would give Whit a day of rest.

We had a couple of days before we could climb any further, so we bunkered in and talked late into the night, listening to Mike's stories about his Vietnam days.

The temperatures dropped severely that night. On such occasions, a practical measure mountaineers employ for additional warmth has to do with a plastic bottle with a large "X" on it. This is a bottle you never want to drink from because, well, it is used in the middle of the night when traveling to the restroom sounds unappealing. Filled with its warm body temperature fluid, my little bottle served as a nice heater at the bottom of my sleeping bag that evening.

The next morning I strolled over to the ranger tent where I met Jim. We sat around his tent drinking hot chocolate and talking about the many moods of Denali. As a ranger, he knew some harrowing stories.

"You can't be too careful on old Denali," Jim warned. "A couple of years ago a friend of mine from Poland named Cristoff tried going solo to the summit. A storm hit as he started back down. He'd only gone one or two hundred feet from the top when he was forced to stop and dig a snow cave. Since he'd intended to make the summit in one day, he hadn't brought along his stove or the sleeping gear he needed to bivouac on the mountain."

No matter how often the rangers and veteran climbers told their war stories, I listened with rapt attention. If I learned from the mistakes of others I might not have to learn the hard way.

Jim continued, "No one had seen or heard from him since he hiked out of camp. On the third day the weather broke, and I immediately sent out an air rescue team. The pilot of the plane spotted him coming out of his snow cave, alive. They radioed to base for a helicopter to airlift him out. He lost both legs below the knee from frostbite." Jim cleared his throat. "He's living in Anchorage. Meeting you would be really encouraging."

"Give me his name and phone number. I'll be glad to talk with him."

Early the next morning we awakened to the roar of a helicopter circling overhead. I stuck my head out of the tent to see what was happening, but the low cloud ceiling obstructed my view of the chopper. I called to one of the hikers we spoke with the previous night. "What's happening out there?"

He paused, his eyes filled with anguish. "The two Koreans—the rescue team found them."

"And?" I knew the answer, but I had to ask anyway.

He shook his head and bit his lip. "It's bad. Really bad."

His words spiraled inside of my head. "It's bad. Really bad." My hands shook as I crawled out of my sleeping bag. I dug my clothing out from the bottom of it, strapped on my prosthesis, and stuck my other foot into my plastic boot. It had frozen solid during the night and felt like putting my foot into a bag of ice cubes.

Whit, whose sleeping bag was next to mine, grunted and burrowed deeper into his bag. However Adrian, who was on the other side of Whit, sat up sleepily. "What's happening?"

"They found the Korean climbers." My voice caught in my throat, for even though I never met the men, we were kin – brothers facing the same odds, but hopefully not the same fate. "The chopper's coming to take their remains off the mountain."

I hopped out of the tent and hurried over to join the silent assembly of climbers watching the rescue team load the two body bags into the helicopter. I shuddered as the helicopter lifted off, one body bag draped over the pilot's lap, where it would be for the entire flight off the mountain.

"Imagine flying all the way to Anchorage with a dead body resting in your lap," I whispered.

One of the veteran climbers kicked at the snow by his feet. "Sometimes, when they can't fly in to retrieve the bodies, they store them in the snow until it's safe for the chopper to land."

"So, what happened to them?" I asked the man nearest me.

"As much as the rangers can piece together, the storm moved in and they didn't have the necessary gear with them. Instead of hunkering down to weather out the storm, they headed back across Headwall." He swallowed hard. "Both of them were found frozen to death. One was dangling from his rope, upside-down. The other was sitting on a rock with his radio next to his head, as though he was trying to call someone."

Rocky caught up to me on the way back to our campsite. "Man, what a bummer."

I nodded but couldn't reply. I couldn't stop thinking of the two men's families and the grief they would soon be experiencing. The faces of my mom and dad surfaced before my eyes. I knew they anxiously awaited the news of my successful ascent on the Great One. All the doubts I had before beginning the climb returned, bringing with them an array of gruesome new considerations. The fact that the Koreans had died a short distance from where I stood, on the same path I was getting ready to take, was not lost on me.

I desperately needed a sense of peace because I felt enveloped by fear. I walked away from everyone to find solitude.

Before long, the words of my friends, Fred and Kathy, came back to me.

"You'll do fine," I remembered Fred's encouraging voice. "The Headwall is steep, but you can make it."

Kathy seconded his thoughts, "You're going to be fine, Todd. Just go up there and have fun."

I also thought of all the comfort and encouragement Lisa gave me when I called her from the 7,200-foot base camp.

I choked back a wave of emotions.

I felt a deep sense of gratitude for God and His angels, who I knew were watching over me and protecting me, even in this remote land. Death had occurred on the path directly ahead of me, but I knew I could trust in this greater power and move forward with the faith that got me this far.

CHAPTER NINETEEN

17,000 Feet High

A somber atmosphere permeated camp that night. I kept seeing those body bags as I prepared to sleep.

Whit was especially quiet since the helicopter left. As we climbed into our sleeping bags, he said, "Seeing those body bags today sure brings home how dangerous it really is up here."

It was surprising to hear Whit, the guy with the fearless I-can-do-anything attitude, talk like that.

The next morning, as we prepared for the climb to 17,200 feet, Rocky stopped by our tent.

"Thought you and your buddies might want to chow down on these leftovers," he offered.

Did we ever! He was part of a well-respected guide company that cooked for their climbers. We were grateful he thought about us and our dehydrated packages of food he had seen us eating. Though Rocky was raised around a lot of money, I could tell by the way he handled various situations on the mountain he had a huge heart for helping others.

After a quiet breakfast, we roped up – Mike in front, then me, Whit, and Adrian on the end. Gliding my hand over the metal climbing gear, I adjusted the harness around my waist for comfort. It took us an hour to gear-up and leave camp.

With great effort, we began up the mountain. The low ceiling of clouds lifted, and for the first time we could see the other side. Row upon row of magnificent mountains and valleys stretched eastward, all lathered with snow and glistening in the midday sun.

Any levity this image conjured up disappeared when we passed the spot where the bodies of the two Koreans were discovered. We stopped for a moment. I said a silent prayer for them, their friends, and family.

We moved on silently.

In the distance, people climbing the Headwall looked like a row of ants carrying food back to their hill. I had watched hikers travel up and down on it from a distance for days. As we got closer, it seemed even more formidable – especially with the yawning crevasse at the base.

The Headwall was the section Whit struggled with when he, Mike, and Adrian were taking our gear to 16,800. It is the steepest part of the climb, and is nine hundred feet of hard ice covered by light snow.

We strapped on our crampons, pulled out our ice axes, and attached our jumars to the ropes placed there by the climbing rangers.

Jumars are metal handles that help you shimmy up the mountain. They move freely up the rope, but lock down when pressure is applied. Looking into the frozen jaws of the crevasse below, I knew how important it was to maintain focus.

Toe by toe, inch by inch, I moved. The dull thud of the ice axe secured each step, pulling my weight up to the next level. Once again, my upper body strength played to my advantage, and I made it to the top with relative ease.

The view was astounding. The mountain represented a power and force too awesome for humans, a spiritual experience too intricate to describe. I felt insignificant and fragile beyond words.

I realized mastery of the peaks took more than a sound heart and lungs. To drive the legs and body beyond fatigue level took a personal resolve, a determination, a positive inner spirit or force. I saw the climb from this point forward would be much more about mental attitude than physical strength, yet both would be required.

We edged along the West Buttress on our way to our gear at 16,800. The goal was to grab it and continue up to the 17,200 camp.

As I began the toe-to-toe climb along the steep, narrow ridge made of rock and wind-packed snow, I realized it wasn't the excitement of climbing the high peaks, or the flirtation with danger, motivating me. It was the desire to challenge the walls society, or perhaps I, myself, had built around me.

Here, in the mountains, I was discovering myself – limits to my endurance, the spirit driving me beyond those limitations, and the power residing in my innermost being. The box created out of my doubts and fears and the well-meaning but restricted views others had of me – I was leaving it behind. Not only was I going out of the box, I was realizing I was never created to be in a box in the first place. I was entering a world in which boxes and limitations didn't exist. A no box world.

We moved at a fast pace, but Mike wanted to move faster to make sure we reached our 17,200 goal.

I was getting a different message.

My inner voice was warning me to stop and rest. I remembered Vern and Jim's warnings to take it slow. I got the feeling we needed to go back to an area just above the Headwall to make camp. From a logistical standpoint this made no sense. We hadn't climbed for long that day and had the physical wherewithal to make it much farther. Furthermore, the area at 16,000 was narrow and not at all conducive to camping, whereas high camp at 17,200 was a large field, similar to 14,200. Finally, our gear was at 16,800, and if we turned around now we'd have to make camp with only the gear on our backs.

Regardless, I learned long ago not to argue with my inner voice, so I spoke up.

"Hey guys – I'm getting a feeling we need to go back to 16,000 and camp."

"Are you kidding? That makes no sense!" Whit argued. "We really need to keep going."

Adrian tapped the tip of his ski pole against a snow mound, "Yeah, I agree."

With the wind off another glacier whipping up the side of the mountain, I found a rock where I could sit and get a drink. My tongue felt as though it had been swabbed with a cotton ball. I took a swig from my water bottle, savoring the relief the cold liquid gave my throat.

"Don't go on any farther today," the voice inside said again. Everything in me cried, "Stop!"

However I knew I couldn't just tell these guys we needed to turn back because of a gut feeling, or an inner voice I was hearing. That wouldn't fly. Unless there was a rock-solid reason to turn around, backtracking was insanity in their books.

"I don't feel we should go farther. It isn't that I'm blown out, but I think I need to take it slower. I need to conserve my leg for the summit attempt."

Adrian spoke up, "Look, Todd, I can't take much more time off from work to do this climb. We need to get it done so I can get back."

"I know, but I feel it's important we not move too fast." I tried to explain my reasoning. "Think about it. There are two advantages to setting up camp at 16,000. If a storm materializes, we'll be much safer there. All we'd have to do if we needed supplies is hurry back down the Headwall to the camp at 14,200. But if we continue on, Whit and I could get weaker from our altitude sickness, and there's nobody to help us at 17,200."

"And the second?" asked Mike.

"The second is, if the storm doesn't materialize, we'll be starting out fresh and ready for that last push to the summit."

They still weren't convinced.

I knew I had to take my stand. "I'm not comfortable with going on. Something is telling me to go back to set up camp. This is my expedition, and I say we go back."

Whit and Adrian urged me to reconsider, but I didn't budge.

Irritated, Mike slapped his gloves against his pant leg and strode away.

Despite the tension now building between the rest of my team and me, I had to listen to the inner voice I'd come to know and trust. I knew effective leaders sometimes have to make unpopular decisions and stick with them.

Whit and Adrian would not meet my gaze as they did an about-face to head back to 16,000.

Our Army Sargent was not so quiet about his displeasure. He let me know, with an array of colorful language, just how unpopular my decision was.

We hadn't gone far when it hit. A storm came out of nowhere and beat down upon us like a hammer.

Whiteout conditions left me completely blind, and my ice axe and crampons struggled to do their job.

The wind slammed against me, going right through my sub-arctic clothing, and my legs started to freeze.

I called out to Mike, Whit, and Adrian, but my voice was silenced by the screaming of the fierce storm.

I felt completely helpless.

I reached for the rope – my team's lifeline.

We slowly made our way to each other.

Fortunately we were close to where we needed to set up camp, and since the area sat at a slightly different angle on the mountain and on the other side of a ridge, the wind was blocked enough for us to see.

We set up the only tent we had and burrowed inside.

That evening we listened to the weather report on the radio. The storm that hit was a Baltic Sea storm, and these were known to last four or five days. I remembered hearing about thirteen climbers who died in one last year.

We awakened to another day of total whiteout conditions. Except for the constant whistle of the wind, we were trapped in a colorless, silent, surrealistic world of vacuous white. We had nowhere to go and nothing to do but stay in our tent, wrapped up in our sleeping bags.

Mike stated, "I'm glad we stopped."

This gave me a new respect for him. It showed a great deal of character to swallow his pride and admit someone else was right, especially when that person was the less experienced climber.

The hours passed slowly.

Occasionally hikers stumbled down from 17,200. Their comments were all the same. "We're bailing. It's miserable up there! Much colder. The winds could blow you off the side of the mountain."

Many groups had run out of food and were physically depleted. Their survival instincts had eclipsed their desire to summit.

The Peter Pan Expedition team came by our camp with someone from another team who had a severely injured hip. He had to be carried down to 14,200 so he could be airlifted off the mountain. They were unselfishly forfeiting their summit attempt and would have to try again next year. I felt their disappointment as though it was my own, but to me, they were true heroes. They placed the well-being of a total stranger ahead of their own goals and dreams.

Before leaving our camp they gave us their extra cache of food. Other groups did the same. It made more sense than carrying the unnecessary weight or abandoning it to the elements. We were appreciative. Every little bit helped.

One guy who had climbed all of the other forty-nine high points lumbered by. "Denali is not my mountain. I'm going home."

He was one mountain shy of hiking all fifty, and was so close to the summit.

I thought about the hopes dashed by the storm and hoped we wouldn't be taking our own march of defeat down the mountain. Thanks to the other teams that had given us their food, we most likely had the means to wait it out.

However I couldn't shake the oppressive atmosphere that seemed to be infecting the mountain. It began with the news of the Koreans, and continued with the presence of the storm. My thoughts began to feel disjointed and unreal.

Alone in the tent, I took time to pray. I silently and humbly turned to God. "I know my motives for doing this expedition are rooted in your Love and Power, otherwise I never would have made it this far. It is what has supplied me with everything I've needed, regardless of the challenges that have arisen. And I know your hand would not have carried me this far, this close to the finish line, to simply fail. I have turned this expedition over to you, and will continue to do so. I'm trusting in your goodness to see it through."

As had become my experience when turning to God, I felt a wave of peace wash over me.

That night the temperatures dropped to what seemed like minus fifty degrees. We had chosen to leave Mike's tent at the 14,200 camp to lighten our packs, so all four of us had to pile into my three-man tent. Whit, Adrian, and I slept feet to head, while Mike stretched out across the bottom of the tent.

Cramped by the crowded conditions, I lay motionless in my sleeping bag for several hours, unable to get comfortable. The close quarters also made it obvious none of us had showered in two weeks. The smell was powerful.

157

The following morning we awoke to cloudless blue skies and pristine white snow – a perfect day for climbing.

"It's a short climb today," Adrian assured me as I adjusted my crampon onto my plastic boot.

After roping up, we headed for the ridge. I used my ice axe for balancing and self-arrest.

I paused to catch my breath when we were half-way up. I gazed down the sharp drop-off from the ridge to the valley below. I appreciated being roped up to three other people who could stop my fall should it occur.

Adrian and Whit drew closer. Mike waited up ahead. We met a few other climbers along the way, but the mountain was basically ours to enjoy.

"Are we almost there?" I asked as I took a long drink from my water bottle.

"It's not far," both Whit and Adrian assured me.

"Good." I tucked my water bottle into my pack and set out once more.

Each time I stopped to rest, they gave me the same answer, "It's not far. We're almost there."

After the fourth time of hearing that answer, I finally caught on. It was like reliving the car vacations I took when I was a kid and repeatedly asked my parents if we were there yet.

My head was starting to ache from the altitude, but I couldn't take the medication the doctor gave me until we reached the camp at 17,200.

Once we finally arrived, the view took us all by surprise. With the exception of one tent, it was a ghost camp. Instead of clusters of tents, the snow walls surrounded emptiness. Nobody had known when the storm would break, so every team except one bailed when there was a break in the weather. If only they waited one more day.

While Whit, Adrian, and I set up camp, Mike feverishly tried to light the stove, but the lack of oxygen and strong winds made it impossible. Without a stove to cook food and melt snow for drinking water, we'd be in deep trouble.

I tried not to appear anxious during the half-hour he worked on it. Apparently the calm I saw on the others' faces was a facade as well, because all four of us breathed a huge sigh of relief when the burner finally caught fire.

The cup of hot chocolate I savored moments later tasted delicious.

The exhaustion and stress from the events of the last few days precipitated shorter tempers than usual. In addition, the next day was the big one – the day we would attempt to summit – and the disagreements about climbing strategies elevated the tension between us.

Living quarters in our tent seemed even more crowded that night than previous nights. No one was in the mood to swap stories.

As I stared up at the dome over our heads, watching it frost over with our breath, my thought ruminated over the one question constantly gnawing at me.

Would we be able to make the summit?

We still had some incredible obstacles to hurdle.

I shut my eyes and burrowed deep into my sleeping bag in an effort to escape the bone numbing chill. Next to me, Whit grunted in his sleep. Adrian mumbled some unintelligible words. Mike nudged my foot as he shifted his weight. All three were asleep, and I was wide awake.

I pulled out the tape recorder that was my faithful companion throughout the expedition and whispered into it, "This is it. Tomorrow's the big day."

Above my face, the tent dome billowed and shuddered in the howling sub-Arctic winds.

"They're calling for another major storm," I continued, "but the sky is looking clear. If it stays this way it will be a perfect day for a summit pitch." I turned it off and stowed it safely in my pack.

During the night, the condensation from our breathing rose to the top of the dome, froze on the interior of our tent, and then snowed back down on us. I tried to ignore it by burrowing even deeper into my sleeping bag, but the snow kept stealing its way down my shirt.

When morning finally arrived, we ate breakfast and prepared for the day's climb. Conversation was minimal.

Mike's words from the previous day played back in my head, "Tomorrow will be the hardest day of your life."

My mind flashes back to that fateful day when I was fourteen. "The second hardest."

In spite of the tension, I was pumped. This was the big day! I leaned back and gazed at the blue cloudless sky over my head – perfect! My stomach churned with anticipation.

By 8:30 we were on the trail. Mike set a fast pace across a long snow field at the base of Denali Pass, and Whit and Adrian went past me and followed him. I tried to match their pace, but couldn't, and fell farther and farther behind. I knew I had to take it slow or I wouldn't make it, and the climb and everything it stood for would be lost.

My enthusiasm began to dissipate and I couldn't focus. I wondered if Mike, Whit, and Adrian had reached the point of only caring about attaining the summit for themselves, regardless of the fact that this was supposed to be a team effort with a specific purpose.

We crossed two hundred yards of the field when I stopped and stuck my ice axe into the snow.

"Hey! Remember me?" I shouted, "Remember the reason we're climbing this mountain?"

The three of them turned around and plodded back to where I stood.

"Look, we can't go on climbing this way," I said. "We're out of sync with one another. We need to operate as a team." I steadied myself on the handle of my ice axe. "You guys are setting too fast a pace, and I can't do it."

"Well," Mike stated, "if you feel like you're not able to make it, the three of us can go on to the top without you. With Whit completing every climb, you could still say the Summit America Expedition set a new fifty peaks record."

"No!" I shook my head vehemently, feeling the struggles of the last twenty years building inside.

I spoke slowly and clearly, looking at each of them square in the eyes. "That won't do. The object of this climb is for a disabled person to break the record. The message people need to hear is no challenge is impossible to overcome, regardless of what they've been through. That will only work if I, an amputee climber, not Whit, an able-bodied climber, make it to the top. This is more than just another climb or another record broken. And the three of you, your job is to see the goal is reached."

To reiterate the finality of my position, I spoke the words I knew would pierce through any lingering indecision, "We've got to get this right, or

I'm turning around right here and now."

If I did that, one of them would have to go with me. I considered the risks and decided I had little choice.

"I'm serious. Either you gauge your pace to mine and we work as a team, or it's over."

CHAPTER TWENTY

Summit!

Several moments of silence passed. I read the expressions on Whit, Adrian, and Mike's faces and sensed they were struggling. We all knew if I decided to turn back, one of them would have to return with me, leaving only two to complete the climb, a dangerous journey under the best of circumstances, and foolish considering the storms passing through the area. And if we all turned back now, there wouldn't be another chance to summit.

Adrian exhaled sharply. "OK, we'll keep going. Anytime you need to slow down let us know."

"Fine. The team's motivating factor is that everyone completes the ascent, right?" I searched each of their faces for answers.

They consented.

"Great! Let's get going." I'd been through enough with these guys to know they weren't selfish. Fatigue was trying to suck the best out of all of us, but I couldn't let it.

Throughout the climb to the top of Denali Pass, Mike set an easy pace. We rested at the top, then continued up a short, extremely icy slope.

As we crossed the area known as the Football Field, we talked about being the first team to summit on June 1. We groaned when another team passed us halfway across the field.

At the other side, I stopped and stared up. I'd heard of Pig Hill, but what I saw left me speechless.

"Is that it?" I asked in hushed tones.

"That's it," Mike answered. "Pig Hill."

Pig Hill, with its steep slope, would be a killer at any altitude, but at 19,000 feet? It seemed impossible. However, there was no way I was going to let fear or discouragement stop me this close to the summit.

On the way up the eastern slope of Pig Hill, an aching numbness crept into my back muscles. My good leg throbbed with pain. My stump did the same. I pushed the pain to the back of my mind and concentrated on putting one foot in front of the other.

I slammed my ice axe into the mountain and leaned into it. I thought about my mission, and the message burning within me to come out. I knew I had to finish this climb, or no one would ever hear it.

Before long, I had a formula. Take three breaths, take a step, stop and rest. Take three breaths, take a step, stop and rest. Over and over I repeated the pattern.

The lack of oxygen was taking its toll on my body. Extreme fatigue quivered deep inside me. I inhaled a ragged gulp of air.

My good leg and my stump each floundered like noodles. I hated the slow going. My mind created a scheme that saw me scrambling up the side of the wall like a kid scaling monkey bars. My body mocked the very idea. Pushed beyond anything I had imagined during all my months of training, the wicked wall threatened to break me.

I willed my legs to become impersonal objects, unattached from the rest of me. Hauling the axe out of the snowbank, I slammed it into a higher point on the wall and took another step. My heart pounded against my chest as an unseen power forced the air from it. I slammed the axe against the mountain again.

"You will not win!" I challenged the mountain. "You will not destroy me!" I took another labored step. Each step, I repeated, "I will make it to the top!"

I wrestled all thoughts of defeat from my mind. Something greater than me was getting me up this mountain.

The words of a fellow hiker echoed in my brain. "Pig Hill is really tough, takes everything out of you, a purely psychological battle to get yourself up it. And once you get to the top, you look ahead and realize there's another climb to reach the summit."

Winning the war sounded so cerebral when we were sitting around a camp stove drinking hot chocolate.

"But don't get discouraged," the climber continued. "The last thrust is deceiving. It's really only a short walk, even though it looks long. Get past Pig Hill, and the rest is easy."

His words echoed in my thought, encouraging me. The rest is easy. The rest is easy.

I kept my mind focused on each successive step, and my eyes on the crunched snow packed down by previous climbers. I clambered toward the top of the wall. Every step of the last hundred yards felt like a grenade of pain exploding in my legs.

Suddenly I hit a soft spot in the snow, postholed, and fell. I sat still for a few moments, gathering my senses.

It hurt to breathe the cold air – my nose burned like it did when I had the tubes in it after the boating accident. Breathing through my mouth turned it into a desert, and my tongue felt like a grapefruit and I my runny nose left icicles on my mustache.

I forced myself to get up. "I will not quit! I will not give up!"

I was in knee-deep snow. I leaned on my ice axe with both hands and struggled to my feet. I had to make it. I had to do whatever it took, or my message would never be heard.

With each step, a fresh spasm of hot pain exploded in my foot, and another seared the end of my stump. My lungs threatened to burst with every breath. My heartbeat drummed against my temples to the rhythm of my pain.

At the moment I felt I had reached my limit, Whit pointed, "There it is! There's the summit!"

I gazed in awe at what lay ahead. The summit seemed indomitable. "We still have to go that much higher and farther?"

Then I remembered the climber's words, "It's just an easy walk."

And it was.

On my left was the slope of Pig Hill, and on my right was a razor edge running into a 3,000-foot sheer cliff.

Whether due to the gradual ascent, or the adrenaline pulsating through my body, I was able to maintain a steady pace along the ridge at 20,000 feet. A world of sunshine, blue sky, and sparkling snow spread out before me.

To give my mind something to think about, I identified the different mountains of the Alaskan Range I could see: Mount Foraker, the second highest mountain to Denali; Mount Hunter, known by natives as "Begguya" or, "Denali's child"; and Denali's North Summit, which sits eight hundred fifty feet shorter than the South Summit toward which I climbed. Separated by the Harper Glacier, the two peaks stand about three-and-a-half miles apart.

To the west of us, fat, puffy clouds billowed over the horizon. While they looked friendly, I knew within a half-hour's time we could be trapped in the midst of a life-or-death storm. At that altitude, there was no mercy.

Yet, somehow, I knew it would not reach us.

The exquisite scenery infused me with the energy to keep walking. Step after step the tension within me built as the summit loomed closer. My artificial foot slipped off the path. I struggled to my feet and continued climbing.

Up ahead, Mike turned and raised his hands in triumph.

I accelerated my pace.

"Here it is!" Mike shouted.

I lunged up the last few feet of the mountain. My eyes caught the glint of the sun off some small flags left by the expedition that passed us. They announced the attainment of our goal.

We made it to the high point of North America.

"Yeah! Thank you, God!" My shout filled every crevasse and canyon in Denali National Park. Dizzy from the altitude and the victory, I took a deep breath. The bitter cold air rumbled through my lungs, then out again.

I made it! I accomplished my goal – I conquered the highest and the toughest of the fifty mountains!

It was hard to imagine people traveling from around the world, some losing their life, just to stand on this little square foot of snow.

Was it worth it? Yes!

If I live to be one hundred years old, I will never forget the moment I reached that summit.

Dizzy with excitement, I posed for pictures, and exclaimed, "William Todd Huston. You did it!"

By the grace of God, I beat the odds. A wave of emotion washed over me, and my eyes filled with tears. I swallowed hard and looked away from Mike. Even after inhaling several times, I still wasn't much in control of my feelings.

I was standing on the top of Denali. Mount McKinley as some would say. Me. An amputee, who doctors thought would never walk again, on top of the entire North American continent.

CHAPTER TWENTY-ONE

The Hard Road Down

As far as the eye could see, sun glinted off the snow in a progression of blues and whites. Wanting never to forget the experience, I tried to imprint this majestic sight of mountain after snowcapped mountain into my mind. They dominated the horizon.

Mike stepped up beside me, "This makes it all worth the effort, huh?"

I searched for an adequate word or gesture to express myself, but it was impossible to verbalize the depth of emotions I was feeling at that moment. This summit represented so many goals and ambitions that I could barely think straight.

The rest of the team joined us. Adrian thumped me on the back. "You did it. The hardest mountain is won. You have a great chance to break my record."

He was right. The team always viewed Denali as the mountain that could ultimately prevent us from setting a new world record.

Exuberant over our victory, the four of us danced and shouted and congratulated one another like a varsity football team after a big win.

Maybe it was just the excitement, but suddenly I wasn't cold at all.

"I expected it to be much colder up here," I called out to Mike.

He glanced down at the thermometer on his watch. "It's not bad, only ten degrees."

"Above or below zero?" I asked.

"Below."

"You're right, Todd. It feels warmer than that to me, too" Whit agreed.

He wiped his gloved hand across his nose, where he found the mucous from it frozen onto his face. "Well, I guess it's colder than I thought." We all laughed.

Before long I began to shiver from the sweat I worked up during the climb.

"We better not stay here too long." Mike drove his ice axe into the snow by his feet. "Let's get a few more snapshots and head back down before the next storm hits."

We got pictures of the summit, of one another holding victory banners, and of the spectacular scenery surrounding us. Every direction I looked brought a new rush of emotion.

I never wanted this moment to end. I never wanted it to slip from my memory. I took one last three hundred sixty-degree pan of the world atop the Great One. I stared at the frozen world, sprawling in muted splendor beneath me. For a moment, nothing else stirred. I breathed deeply, then let it out slowly as the solitude of the mountain engulfed me. The whir of a light breeze soothed my senses, lulling me into an exquisite sense of contentment and peace. It was as if the entire world was holding its breath for us.

I remembered the months of hard work Whit, Lisa, and I had put into *Summit America*. With a deep sense of gratitude, I thought about all of the people who supported and prayed for me and this expedition. It was all worth it.

"Thank you, God," I whispered.

We finally started to feel the frigid temperatures seeping through our Arctic clothing, reminding us we were visitors, not residents. It was time to begin the long descent back toward civilization. For all the exhilaration I felt conquering the highest point in North America, it wouldn't mean much if I didn't make it back to civilization alive. And really, I was only halfway there. I still had to climb down the mountain. With my energy drained and my legs in bad shape, it wouldn't be easy.

I looked at my watch and was astounded to realize we had been there for an hour. It only seemed like fifteen minutes. We needed to leave immediately, for our safety.

The trip down would be a lot shorter – only two days, compared to the twelve-day ascent. However, as climbers know, and as I found on the lower forty-eight, the descent is always harder.

I didn't realize the extent of my exhaustion until I took my first steps downward. If I thought my legs were like noodles before, this was worse. Gritting my teeth, I focused my thoughts on the path.

We completed the first part of the descent quickly and with relative ease before we started down Pig Hill.

I took a few steps, and then, squish. My artificial leg postholed into the snow. Before I could recover my balance, the trail broke away, propelling me sideways down the wall.

In a blur I was flailing in the air, grabbing for the rope attached to my climbing belt. Why wasn't the rope holding me? I could sense my falling body gaining speed. Snow-sky-snow-sky. I tumbled faster and faster.

"Todd!" I could hear my climbing partners shouting.

"It's all over!" I thought in a moment of detachment. "So this is what it's like to…"

Suddenly, the rope jerked taut. I skidded to a halt and, for a moment, stared at the cascades of loose snow tumbling down into the valley below. Recovering my senses, I jammed my ice axe into the snow pack and hauled myself back onto the trail.

I rested for a moment, my breath coming in short, agonizing spurts. Pain shot through my legs as I struggled to my feet. I pulled my artificial leg up and took another step.

Suddenly, I postholed again. Again I tumbled from the trail. Rolling onto my stomach, I fought my way to my feet once more, only to tumble again. My pack hung heavy on my shoulders. A numb ache crept into the muscles up and down my spine. The pain behind my eyes increased. I longed to stop and rest.

The sunlight had softened the snow on the trail creating prime conditions for postholing. Every few steps my artificial leg broke through the crust and sent me sprawling down the mountainside. I struggled to my feet after each fall, focusing my attention on the trail before me. I wanted to pray for strength, but the pain in my body was overriding my thinking process.

A war commenced inside my head – against my body's cries of protest and demands for unconditional surrender.

I smiled through my pain, determined. The grueling pace continued.

"Just one more step," I told myself. But as I took it, my artificial leg postholed again, pitching me face-first into the snow. Saturated with sweat and in agony, I rolled over and wiped the snow from my goggles. I looked at the sapphire blue sky above me, defeated.

CHAPTER TWENTY-TWO

Cheers Through the Pain

I felt like I never wanted to get up again and couldn't go on any longer.

Through blurred eyes, I gazed at the endless white-capped mountain peaks surrounding me.

Above me, I could hear Mike and Adrian's voices, "Todd, are you all right? Did you break something?"

With my foot constantly postholing, it was taking more energy to get down this mountain, and it was beating the heck out of me.

"You are not letting yourself quit," I whispered. "After everything you have accomplished today, and the mission you have to fulfill, this is not going to stop you." I felt strength within building, and proclaimed out loud, "Just suck it up and do it Todd!"

This journey started with one step, and that's what was going to finish it – quitting was not an option.

When I got up, determined to take another step, something changed inside of me. Call it a second wind. Call it a change in my attitude. Whatever it was, it was as if my mind detached from my body and the pain and fear wrecking it. All thoughts of quitting vanished. All thoughts of failure disappeared.

It hit me that fear doesn't exist. Any fear seeming to engulf me during this expedition, and throughout my life, only had the power I gave it in my thinking. Dangers exist, but I didn't need to fear them. I needed to work through them with clear, logical thinking, and fear would only fog productive thinking.

I still hurt, but it was as if an outside source of energy propelled me slowly, steadily down the trail. Slipping, postholing, falling, snow building up on my crampons – all of that remained the same, but I had changed.

When we reached Denali Pass, Mike set up snow stakes to act as anchors to control our descent. This was the spot where the soldier and his girlfriend fell after their summit.

Keeping an eye on the crevasse below, we climbed carefully down the slope. No one was in the mood for risks.

As we neared the 17,200-foot base camp, Adrian stayed to walk with me while Whit and Mike hurried ahead to start the camp stove.

As I hiked the last few steps into camp I felt wiped out. I tossed my gear onto the ground and fell onto my sleeping bag.

During the next hour I groaned every five or ten seconds from the pain pulsating through my body. I tried to disassociate my mind from it, a technique I learned when I was in the hospital after my leg injury, but it didn't work. I took a couple of Advil and burrowed down inside my sleeping bag.

One last conscious thought nagged at me as I drifted off to sleep. I wondered how in the world I'd be ready to climb the rest of the way down.

I awakened to the whine of an airplane buzzing our tent. I looked at my watch and saw it was 3:00 a.m. I wondered why he was up here at this time of night. I later learned he picked up a climber at a lower camp who had developed cerebral edema, a swelling on the brain caused by high altitude. Fortunately they got him to the hospital on time and he was OK.

The next morning when I crawled out of my tent I felt really good. I stretched my arms – no pain in my back muscles. I flexed my good leg – no pain. I massaged my stump, still no pain. I was ready to roll!

We roped up, adjusted our crampons, and headed toward our first goal, 14,200 camp.

It was hard going. The sun and high winds were brutal going down the Headwall, but I soon adjusted to the rhythm. I couldn't walk down it sideways like the other guys because my crampon wouldn't stay attached to my artificial foot, so I backed down, hoping I wouldn't accidentally step into a hidden crevasse.

We took it slow across the ice field and down the avalanche area. Cautiously, we circumvented the open crevasses, until we finally arrived, alive, at 14,200.

I threw my hands into the air and gave an Oklahoma cheer, "Yahoo!"

What a great feeling it was to be back in civilization again. While Whit and the others set up camp, I shed my gear, pulled on my down jacket, and walked to the ranger's tent.

"Hey, Jim," I called from outside his entryway.

"Come on in."

I didn't need a second invitation. I burst into the tent, shouting, "We did it! We summited."

Jim leaped up from the table where he and three guests were eating. "Wonderful!" he shouted with a high-five.

I beamed all over. "It's beautiful up there! Absolutely breathtaking."

"I told you. There's nothing like it. You'll never be the same again."

"You've got that right." Then I thought of something. "Is it possible for me to make a phone call from here?"

"You bet. Make yourself comfortable." He offered me a chair and returned to his guests.

I called Lisa from my cell phone. I could barely control my excitement when I heard her answer.

"Lisa! We did it! We made it!"

"What?" I heard the excitement building in her voice.

"We made it! We're back at the 14,200 camp. We did it! Can you believe it?" I choked back a wave of emotion.

"Congratulations! I never doubted for a minute you would!" She paused for a moment. "But that was fast – I didn't expect to hear from you for another week."

"It was fast, wasn't it? It was an amazing team effort, and I suppose you could say God was our fifth team member who carried us through!" I laughed. There was no doubt in my mind God's strength and power were the reasons we accomplished that summit. "Do you mind calling everyone? My parents, Fred and Kathy, and anyone else you can think of who'd like to hear the news."

"Sure, I'll be glad to," and again stated, "I knew you could do it!"

"Yes. We did it!" It felt good to repeat those words.

I tried to describe the climb to her – the beauty, the cold, the summit – but realized how hard it was to make someone who'd never been there understand.

After Lisa and I said good-bye, Jim invited me to eat with them. "I'm sure you're hungry for real food by now."

I hesitated. "Are you sure you have enough?"

"Are you kidding? We have plenty. Come on. Pull up your chair and tell us about your climb."

The warm, cozy atmosphere in the heated tent and tantalizing aroma of hot macaroni and cheese melted away any desire to return to my camp. Real food! I couldn't resist.

I wanted to invite my teammates to join us, but they were asleep by the time I got to our camp. I decided to go back to Jim's.

Jim, his guests, and I talked for more than three hours. I shared my life story and goal to inspire others with my message. One of the guests talked about some difficulties he was facing. A women talked about her journey of self-discovery and what she planned to do with her life. It was a wonderful evening sharing ideas.

I returned to my tent and climbed into my sleeping bag. I expected to drift off to sleep immediately, but memories of the last few days kept playing over and over in my head. I remembered what Jim said about never being the same again, and he was right. I smiled as I thought of my friends and family who encouraged me to go for it.

I also thought about events we experience throughout our lives. Some are traumatic, like a boating accident, and some bring us sheer joy, like this expedition. I realized every experience can propel our lives forward, if we let it.

I asked myself if everything I went through was worth it, and decided it absolutely was.

Then the face of my ex-wife surfaced in my mind. I winced. A hard knot of pain filled my throat.

"Oh, God," I breathed.

As quickly as the prayer escaped my lips, a fresh new thought replaced it. Jessie may have gained a country, but I gained the world.

The interviews I had done and the speaking engagements waiting for me when I returned flashed through my mind. I really did gain the world. I had a new mission, and was excited to see how far God would take it!

Late into the night I finally fell asleep.

Morning arrived too soon. Our goal was to beeline it for the Kahiltna Glacier base camp.

At first it was slow going. The two sleds piled high with our gear kept sliding off the trail. We repeatedly had to right them and lift them back onto it. Doing this while roped together was very difficult.

The sun rose in the sky, growing hotter as we descended the mountain. Snow melting on the glaciers created huge rolling hills of snow where flat, level terrain was earlier.

We skirted the places where climbers had punched holes into hidden crevasses along the trail. We could see where hikers had fallen into crevasses and been rescued.

"Look, this is taking forever," Mike announced. "Let's cut the rope. Todd and I will move together on one rope, while you two use the other to maneuver the sleds down the mountain."

"Good idea." Adrian snapped out his pocketknife. "Once we're past this section we'll grab our last cache of supplies at 11,200. With the added weight the sleds will run better and we'll catch up with you in no time."

As soon as it was safe, I stopped to remove my crampons. My good leg was getting sore from jamming against the toe of my plastic boots. Without the traction, however, I slipped down the rest of the slope.

My foot was still throbbing so I stopped at regular intervals to allow the blood to circulate into it. I appreciated how kind and patient Mike was with these delays.

Whit and Adrian caught up with us at 10,000 feet. "We'll keep going," Adrian suggested, "and set up camp at the 8,000-foot level."

I nodded.

As they went on, I stumbled and fell to the ground. Mike helped me to my feet.

"Todd," he said, "I'm sorry about everything up there on the mountain."

"That's OK. I knew that was just the fatigue talking. You've more than made up for it today. I wouldn't be able to do this without you, and I appreciate it."

On our way down Ski Hill we met Brian Okonek, another famous climber. He and his team clapped and cheered for me when we arrived at the 8,000-foot camp, which felt amazing. I couldn't believe people recognized me.

We threw our sleeping bags on the snow and slept four hours. At 3:00 a.m. we woke up and continued heading down the slope. Trekking across the Kahiltna Glacier was much easier while the snow was harder.

When we arrived at the base camp I headed straight for the ranger station.

"Annie!" I burst through the front door. "We did it! We summited."

"Congratulations! I heard the news from Jim this morning." The brown-haired woman with the giant smile jumped up from her desk at the radio controls and gave me a hug. We talked a few minutes about the climb.

"Guess you'll be needing a taxi?" she asked cheerfully.

"Sure will." I grinned. "This morning if possible. Whit and Adrian should be here any minute."

Annie seated herself in front of the short-wave radio and called the air taxi service at Talkeetna International Airport.

"Four more to transport, Jeff," she reported.

"Roger," came the muffled reply.

I waved to Annie and headed out the door.

I made it but a few feet when a stranger approached me. "Hey, aren't you the guy I saw on the news?"

Others joined him.

"Congratulations!"

"Inspiring!"

"Great job!"

Every few feet I posed for pictures with people I'd never met before, people from around the world. Some spoke in languages I couldn't understand, however, their joyous expressions crossed any language barrier.

Whit and Adrian arrived a half-hour behind us. With the clear weather there were no flight delays. Only a strong wind whipped across the wide glacier.

Mike and I boarded the first plane and Whit and Adrian took the second. We bounced down the runway and lifted off into the icy Alaska air.

I watched as the brilliant mountain which had been my home for the last two weeks grew smaller. I was grateful to the Great One for all it taught me. My heart said its final good-bye, and I turned toward to the journey still to come.

CHAPTER TWENTY-THREE

More Than Mountains

I closed my eyes and tried to imagine which of society's conveniences I missed most. Brushing my teeth, shaving, washing my clothes, bathing... I definitely missed bathing the most. We smelled horrible.

It's critical to remain warm on the mountain, so we never removed our clothing regardless of the accumulation of sweat and dirt. Once in a while, we peeled off our thermals if it was too warm, then put them back on when temperatures dropped. Every time we crawled into our sleeping bags, the pungent aroma of body odor was overpowering.

I wanted a hot shower.

Once we landed in Talkeetna, we consolidated our gear into one big package for the taxi service taking us to Anchorage the next day. Sleeping bags, hiking clothes, thermals – everything would have to wait to be washed until we got to Spokane. I hoped for the driver's sake he didn't have a good sense of smell.

In the wonderfully hot shower at the bunkhouse, I closed my eyes, letting the water pulsate against my face and chest. I felt my body beginning to thaw. It took thirty minutes of scrubbing to eradicate the layers of grime and sweat from my skin.

Next came the hair. Three shampoos later, my hair squeaked clean between my fingers.

Finally, I shaved the two weeks' growth of beard from my face.

I examined the finished product in the mirror, and laughed out loud. With the beard gone, I looked like a bandit! I was tan around the eyes and white where the beard had been.

I decided to keep the longer hair as part of my mountain man image.

With a pair of clean blue jeans and a *Summit America* sweat shirt, I was ready to face the world.

Well, almost.

I could barely walk. The ball of my foot hurt terribly and the rest of it was numb. The nails on my big toe and the toe next to it were blistered and black.

I pulled on a pair of heavy socks. I couldn't tolerate the thought of shoes.

I limped over to the telephone and called my parents to tell them the good news. They were elated about my success.

Then I called Fred. His love and commitment were phenomenal throughout this journey. He was the first to encourage me when I considered taking on the challenge alone.

When I heard his voice, I almost choked. "We did it, Fred. We did it."

"I never doubted you would," he proclaimed, without hesitation.

When I hung up, I headed to the general store to get something to eat. My problem was making a decision. After eating dehydrated food for two weeks, everything looked good.

That same day we attended the funeral for the two Koreans who died on the mountain. Parents, wives, children, and friends of the two men, supported by a number of climbers, huddled together as the pastor from the Korean Presbyterian Church in Anchorage spoke a few words over the open caskets.

One of the rangers broke down as he read a poem for his friend, the Korean instructor. I gazed at the grieving faces and thought about the two men – young, vigorous, healthy – whose lives ended so abruptly. They weren't much different from me, except they were more experienced climbers. Once again, I thanked God for my safe return and prayed for those still on the mountain.

When the mourners left, I wandered through the little Talkeetna graveyard, reading the names of climbers who had died on the mountain. Some of them still remained on the mountain, their bodies resting in a bottomless crevasse or isolated glacier.

By good fortune, Cristoff was in town. He was the Polish climber with the amputated legs Ranger Jim told me about. We arranged to have lunch together.

Over a bowl of vegetable soup, Christoff's round, red face became animated as he told me about his ordeal on the Great One.

"Three days the storm battered me. I thought I'd die." He glanced down at his legs, then back at me, "As it is, I lost both legs below the knees." He spoke so matter-of-factly I couldn't help but admire his spirit.

We quickly became friends. I told him about my life and my goal to break the highpoint record. We talked about the emotional impact our amputations had on each of us and how we coped with the loss.

"So, Christoff, where do you go from here?" I asked

"If all goes well, I plan to climb her again next year." His face beamed with the eager anticipation of summiting Denali again.

"That's great, man." Looking at him, I knew it would be tough, but I truly believed he would do it.

During the meal a reporter came to interview me about the climb. I glanced at Christoff during the interview and saw a trace of sadness it wasn't he who was being interviewed. But I felt one day he'd be setting his own records as a double amputee.

The next day we drove to Anchorage, where we took Adrian to the airport so he could get back to work. Good-byes are tough when you've been through an experience like Denali together.

The four of us shook hands and let the novelty of the moment sink in. When he turned to walk toward his gate, I reflected on the selflessness of this extraordinary man. It couldn't have been easy supporting an expedition whose purpose was to break his record, yet he lent his expertise without complaint. I'm sure he figured if someone was to break it, at least it was someone who would use the experience to help others.

Cristoff, who was from Anchorage, invited us over for a Polish meal of stuffed cabbage and potatoes. Some of his friends joined us, and I appreciated seeing how supportive they were of him. We had a great time talking and eating.

Later we enjoyed a delicious Japanese meal at Mike's friends' home. Some of his relatives were there, including nieces and nephews. We were reminded again of his kind, gentle side as we watched him play with them.

We loved all of this tasty food people made for us. It almost made up for the weeks of dehydrated meals we ate on the mountain. If we kept this up, it wouldn't take long for all the weight I lost to find its way back to my waist.

Next it was time to say goodbye to Mike. I gained a great deal of respect for this man while climbing together, and knew he'd remain a valued friend. His tough exterior boasted discipline and strength of character, but beneath it all was a humility and kindness I admired.

The three of us shook hands and said our good-byes.

It was back to the team of two.

We caught a flight to Los Angeles, where Whit and I would stay overnight before flying to Hawaii. After scraping to get by on Denali, even squished business-class seating felt like the lap of luxury,

Unloading our gear at my home, it quickly became obvious our first order of business was to wash our putrid clothing. In some cases, it took as many as three washings to get the body odors out of our polypropylene underwear, pants, and shirts.

When I sniffed the garments, I wasn't sure if they still stunk, or if the odor was simply embedded in my mind.

Though I was hobbling due to my injured toes, I marveled every time I walked across the floor that I was in a real house, walking on a firm foundation.

I read through the last minute instructions Lisa left for me before flying to Hawaii a couple of days earlier.

Whit and I headed to the airport for the last leg of our trip. This destination was worlds different than the freezing climate of Denali.

The long flight over the Pacific provided calm and quiet to reflect on the journey thus far.

I had a new appreciation for the vastness of my country and its exquisite beauty. Green velvet forests with sunlight peeking through tiny pockets within dense canopies; thirsty sun-drenched drylands with their bold rock formations thrusting toward the heavens; the warm, orange sunset blanketing sleepy mountaintops with its cozy alpine-glow; the lonely song of the morning bird sending its gentle wake-up call to the flowers, insects, and animals so they could prepare for the glorious dawning day.

More importantly, I discovered a deeper beauty in humanity. Ranger Annie's helpful spirit; Barbara's drive and zest for life, along with her faithful companion, Kona; the young women yearning to escape the whirlwind of the big city; the burned-out chemical engineer, searching for meaning in life; the children and teens, each scaling their own personal mountains and barriers; all of the climbers I met along the way, with their kindred love of the outdoors and passion for adventure.

Looking out my window as the plane descended I spotted the sandy beaches on the island of Hawaii. I saw palm trees waving in the soft Pacific breeze, azure blue surf lapping the pearly white sand, suntanned people splashing in the surf – a far cry from the deadly ice crevasses of Denali, the stinging black flies of Katahdin, and my unquenched thirst on Guadalupe Peak.

Once in my hotel room, I prepared for my final summit.

How strange those words sounded. The final summit.

I looked around the room and realized I didn't miss electronics at all. I had no desire to tarnish the stillness and peace with television noise.

I pulled my *Hooked on Phonics* T-shirt over my head and strode over to the mirror to comb my hair.

A knock sounded at the door. "Come on, Todd. Lisa told us to get you to the mountain on time."

My little brother Steve, a student at Brown University, flew to Hawaii with my mother for my last climb.

"I'm coming, I'm coming," I told him.

I was filled with a strange languor as I considered facing my last mountain. For more than a year, I anticipated this expedition. I focused every waking moment on my goal of breaking the highpoint record. For months, I trained my body and mind for the rigors of the climb. For weeks, I lived for each new mountain. For days, I thought of nothing but this morning.

My legs were still sore, but I knew it wasn't why I lacked the energy to get going. Maybe I was simply overwhelmed by the gravity of this day.

Steve knocked again, urging me to hurry.

I adjusted the cap on my sun-bleached hair and walked out the door.

Climbing Mauna Kea, Hawaii's 13,796-foot mountain, would have been anticlimactic after Denali or Rainier except for the celebration Lisa planned. She was already at the Hale Pohaku Visitor's Center to finish preparations for last-minute media coverage of my arrival.

I met Lori, the representative from *Hooked on Phonics*, at the car. She transported my mother and Whit to the mountain while my brother and I rode in the back of a friend's pickup truck.

We rode down palm tree-lined boulevards, past luxurious hotels and tourist shops, and through residential areas, some extravagant, some humble. Next came lava beds. Miles of lava beds.

My brother and I reminisced about the adventures we shared during our Boy Scout days. It seemed like such a short time ago and we both had come so far.

The driver of our truck laid on the horn as we rounded the last corner before the visitor's center. Lori, driving the car behind us, did the same. Banners waved over the steps of the center.

"Congratulations Todd Huston! From *Hooked on Phonics*!"

"Congratulations *Summit America* for Breaking the Record!"

The street light poles wore brightly painted posters that read, "Great Job, Todd! You did it!"

Television camera technicians and news reporters swarmed as my brother and I climbed out of the truck bed. Cameras flashed and Hula women draped leis about my neck and kissed me on the cheek.

I did a television interview on the steps of the visitor's center.

"Having an amputation is just like having a loved one die," I explained. "You go through the same stages of grief. All your hopes and dreams have been shattered. Then you learn to accept it and realize it's just another hurdle in life to overcome.

"I see myself as a representative of the forty-three million Americans who, on any given day, are struggling against major illness, a disability, or any other health-related challenge."

I went on to include challenges that couldn't be X-rayed – challenges like divorce, the death of a loved one, being over-weight, or overcoming drug or alcohol addictions.

I continued to smile as the journalist turned toward the camera to wrap up the interview.

"Todd Huston, from California, stands atop our own Mauna Kea. He climbed to the top of the highest peak in each of America's fifty states. Only thirty-two people have ever accomplished this feat, but Huston, the thirty-third, did it in less time. And with fewer legs."

Someone yelled, "Cut!"

The reporter smiled and thanked me for the interview.

We streamed inside the visitor's center and listened to a presentation about the mountain. The ranger explained Mauna Kea is the number-one place in the world to do stargazing.

"Many countries have placed observatories on top of this mountain. The observatory complex is called the Onizuka Center for International Astronomy, after Air Force Lt. Col. Ellison S. Onizuka, who lost his life on the ill-fated *Challenger* flight in 1986."

At the end of the lecture, we climbed into the waiting vehicles for the winding drive to the summit. The greenery grew sparse as we wound our way up the mountain road.

When the pavement ended, we parked the truck and started climbing the steep gravel road to the whir of video cameras. Whit, Steve, Lori, and the video crew hiked with me.

The landscape was loose volcanic ash and resembled artist renderings of Mars. I recalled snippets of the ranger's lecture at the visitor's center in which he quoted Reverend Martin Luther King's famous "mountaintop" speech.

"I've been to the mountaintop, and I've seen the other side," stated Dr. King.

The other side of Mauna Kea is so barren United States astronauts practice driving their moon buggies on its pockmarked terrain.

Upon reaching the parking lot nearest the summit, I found Lisa and my mother waiting by the car. They had driven on ahead rather than climbed.

"Hey, no fair, you two!" I shouted.

Mom laughed. "Only way to go!"

Lisa climbed out of the car. She and my mother joined the procession of hikers climbing the mountain with me. I glanced toward Lisa and noticed tears filling her eyes.

I looked at my watch. It was almost noon.

Ahead of us were the observatory buildings on the summit. The video cameras rolled while I hiked down a short dip, then up the slope to the top.

This was it. We did it.

A wave of emotion swept over me. I accomplished something few thought possible. I had people helping me along the way, and my heart felt an overwhelming sense of gratitude for them.

But there was something much more powerful, throughout my entire life journey, that had never left me, never doubted I would accomplish the task, always encouraged me, and gave me all I needed to the very finish. I shot a look of gratitude skyward for my final routine mountain thank you to God.

"Thank you for making this day possible," I whispered, feeling tears fill my eyes.

I stepped on the little marker officially ending this life-changing journey. It officially ended *Summit America*.

66 days, 22 hours, and 47 minutes.

Me, a leg amputee, did the impossible, and broke the old record by an astounding thirty-five days.

I grabbed Lisa and gave her a big hug. "This wouldn't have happened," feeling the emotion of the moment, "if it weren't for you."

"Pictures!" one of the photographers shouted.

I gestured to Lisa and Whit to join me, and we threw our arms around each other.

The local radio station I interviewed with earlier in the climb wanted another interview, and the photographers filmed me while I talked on the telephone with them.

"Why did you brave the snow and ice, the dizzying heights, and the unbelievable fatigue to break this record?" the radio personality asked.

"It's about more than mountains or mountain climbing," I answered. "I did it to inspire and encourage people. Everyone has challenges. Whether your challenge is physical, like an amputation, or emotional, like the loss of a loved one through divorce or death, the challenge can be overcome through perseverance and trust in God's guidance."

I had given that answer many, many times since the day I first applied to the *50 Peaks Project*. But I never meant it more than I did standing on the summit of Mauna Kea.

"Tell our listeners about your sponsor, *Hooked on Phonics*," he requested.

Again, I related the story of Lisa and her T-shirt stand. "It was honestly a miracle, the way everything came together."

The final question: "And now, what challenge is next for Todd Huston?"

I grinned. "I want to get the message out that by having faith in God and believing in yourself, you can overcome whatever you face in life."

The media frenzy continued for several minutes. When it slacked off, I paused to enjoy the view of Mauna Kea and the tops of clouds spread out below me.

A gentle sense of peace and deep satisfaction swept over me in the stillness of the warm, Hawaiian breeze.

I wondered how I'd ever go back to a normal eight-to-five existence after seeing life from this perspective.

Finally, it was time to leave, to go down the mountain. I couldn't hold on to the moment any longer. I climbed my mountains and saw the other side. I was no longer the naive and untested man who set out across the continent a few months ago in a red Ford pickup truck. I'd dodged thunderstorms, battled blizzards, endured inconceivable pain, and faced my fears through faith in God.

Time after time, when it seemed like the expedition was doomed, He smoothed the way. Time after time, when my body hurt so badly I thought I couldn't take another step, He infused me with the strength to continue. I found I could always count on God, no matter what. This conviction grew more concrete throughout the expedition.

It always started with one step. It had been that way my entire life, especially since the accident. Each first step opened my eyes to an amazing journey, discovering the incredible gift God created me to experience and give to others.

The step from the hospital bed when I was fourteen led to walking again.

The step to have my leg amputated when I was twenty-one strengthened my resolve to lean on God and His immense strength lying within.

The step to stop the pain medication helped me see I could change my life with one choice.

The step to fill out the *50 Peaks Project* application led to regaining my physical abilities.

The step to courageously do the expedition on my own led to *Summit America* and the emergence of a new life-purpose.

The step toward each of the fifty summits led to conquering years of self-doubt and fears.

The step to reach out to individuals throughout the expedition led to the realization my journey is about sharing my message with the world. It is the greatness I was created to live.

"The purpose of my journey is to help each of you realize you, too, have an incredible journey to fulfill." I step in front of the stage lights so I can look into the eyes of my audience. *The screen behind me displays the final picture of Whit, Adrian, Mike, and me standing atop Denali. "And the only person who can take the step to begin it is you.*

"You already have everything you need for your journey. All the strength, power, and wisdom is now within you. You were created with it. You simply need to bring it out to the world so everyone can be blessed by it."

I had taken the audience through everything. The accident, the amputation, Jessie, and finally the laughs and challenges of the expedition.

"'Why me?' The question I asked for years, from the age of fourteen until the day I began my Summit America journey. I finally found my answer, which is why I'm on stage in front of you right now. You, too, will find the answer to your 'why me' question. I can't tell you when you will find it, or what your answer is, but I can tell you when you'll know you've found it, and that's when your answer not only blesses you, but it also blesses others.

"Everyone, including you, is blessed when you are your best. Being less than who you are helps no one. So be the most loving person you can be and put love into everything you do – in every sound you make and every thought you have – and you will change the world. Because, then, it is true your greatness shining out to the world.

"And once you make the decision to take that first step, you're amazing

187

journey of a thousand miles begins."

The joy washing over me as the crowd rises to its feet, filling the auditorium with their cheers, is reminiscent of my Denali summit a couple of months ago. I say a silent thank you to God as I swallow the emotion welling inside.

The "Summit America" journey was over.

It opened my eyes to the greater life journey I've always been on. It's the journey of self-discovery helping me let go of who I thought I was and awaken to who I was created to be.

I'm engulfed with a sense of peace, a sense of home, as I look into the faces of my smiling audience. I know this is it. Inspiring others to embark on their own journey of self-discovery and greatness is who I was created to be. A thrill wells up inside as realize I just took my greatest first step.

Epilogue

I wanted to repeat my message one more time: By having faith in God and believing in the abilities He's given you, you can overcome whatever challenges you face in life.

We all have challenges. Some are physical, like a leg amputation, heart problems, or a hip replacement. Others cannot be so easily seen. The death of a loved one, a divorce or separation, or combating an addiction to alcohol or drugs can throw up barriers that seem unconquerable. But they are not.

The pain is often difficult, whether physical or emotional, but perseverance can make the difference between success and failure. If we're willing to hang on through the seemingly unending pain, we'll find that it is only a brief chapter. The lessons learned and the joy that grows from surviving will last an eternity.

So whatever you are facing, be strong and courageous. You are not alone. God and His human helpers are there for you. Faith is that which is hoped for but not yet seen. Have faith that God is there to help you overcome whatever you face.

See you at the top!

Todd Huston

Rank	State	Peak	Elevation*
1	Alaska	Denali	20,320
2	California	Mount Whitney	14,495
3	Colorado	Mount Elbert	14,433
4	Washington	Mount Rainier	14,411
5	Wyoming	Gannett Peak	13,804
6	Hawaii	Mauna Kea	13,796
7	Utah	Kings Peak	13,528
8	New Mexico	Wheeler Peak	13,161
9	Nevada	Boundary Peak	13,140
10	Montana	Granite Peak	12,799
11	Idaho	Borah Peak	12,662
12	Arizona	Humphreys Peak	12,633
13	Oregon	Mount Hood	11,239
14	Texas	Guadalupe Peak	8,749
15	South Dakota	Harney Peak	7,242
16	North Carolina	Mount Mitchell	6,684
17	Tennessee	Clingmans Dome	6,643
18	New Hampshire	Mount Washington	6,288
19	Virginia	Mount Rogers	5,729
20	Nebraska	Panorama Point	5,426
21	New York	Mount Marcy	5,344
22	Maine	Mount Katahdin	5,268
23	Oklahoma	Black Mesa	4,973
24	West Virginia	Spruce Knob	4,861
25	Georgia	Brasstown Bald	4,784
26	Vermont	Mount Mansfield	4,393
27	Kentucky	Black Mountain	4,139
28	Kansas	Mount Sunflower	4,039
29	South Carolina	Sassafras Mountain	3,554
30	North Dakota	White Butte	3,506
31	Massachusetts	Mount Greylock	3,487
32	Maryland	Backbone Mountain	3,360
33	Pennsylvania	Mount Davis	3,213
34	Arkansas	Magazine Mountain	2,753
35	Alabama	Cheaha Mountain	2,405
36	Connecticut	Mount Frissell	2,372
37	Minnesota	Eagle Mountain	2,301
38	Michigan	Mount Arvon	1,978
39	Wisconsin	Timms Hill	1,951
40	New Jersey	High Point	1,803
41	Missouri	Taum Sauk Mountain	1,772
42	Iowa	Hawkeye Point	1,670
43	Ohio	Campbell Hill	1,549
44	Indiana	Hoosier Hill	1,257

Rank	State	Peak	Elevation*
45	Illinois	Charles Mound	1,235
46	Rhode Island	Jerimoth Hill	812
47	Mississippi	Woodall Mountain	806
48	Louisiana	Driskill Mountain	535
49	Delaware	Ebright Azimuth	442
50	Florida	Britton Hill	345

*Feet above sea level

Glossary

Adrian Crane – Past record holder of U.S. Fifty highpoints and guide on Denali for the Summit America Expedition.

Amputee – The removal of a body extremity usually due to trauma or disease. A leg can be a below-knee (B/K) or an above-knee (A/K) amputation.

Anchor – Where the rope is connected - to rock, ice, etc. – to provide security.

Belaying – The act of using a rope to protect the other climbers from falling.

Bivouac (bivy) – A temporary camp without tents.

Bergschrund – A crevasse, or series of crevasses, at the upper end of a mountain glacier.

Cache – A place for temporary storage of supplies on the mountain.

Carabiner (biner) – A metal oval that can be used to clip and hold climbing gear.

Cornice – An over-hanging wall of snow found on mountain ridges.

Crampons – Metal spikes that are attached to boots to prevent slipping on snow and ice.

Crevasse – A crack found in a glacier which is sometimes hidden under the snow.

Edema – Swelling of the brain (cerebral edema) or lungs (pulmonary edema) with excess fluid.

Glacier – A river of ice that flows slowly down a mountain.

Glissading – A controlled descent down snow or scree covered slopes on your buttocks, using your ice-axe to steer.

Harness – A waist-belt used by climbers to attach to the rope and carry climbing gear.

Hypothermia – A dangerously low body temperature.

Ice axe – A climbing tool used to climb snow and ice, also used as an anchor or to stop a fall.

Jumar (also known as **Ascender**) – A metal device that clamps on the rope which the climber holds to ascend.

Mike Vining – Army Sargent Special Forces mountaineer instructor; climbing guide for Denali, Borah Peak, Gannett Peak, and Granite Peak on the Summit America Expedition.

Phantom Pain – Pain in a limb that has been amputated. For example, leg amputees feel pain in toes or calves after the leg has been amputated.

Prosthesis – An artificial body part, such as a leg or an arm.

Scree – Small rocks that are found on a mountain slope. Hard to ascend but easier to descend. Hikers "ski-the-scree."

Vern Tejas – World-renowned mountaineer who has broken many world records, including fastest ascent of all seven continent high points, each of which he's summited at least ten times; first solo winter ascent of Denali; first solo ascent of Mount Vinson, the highest point in Antartica; and many others.

Volcano Vent – Locations from which lava flows, volcanic materials are erupted, and sulfur fumes escape.

Whit Rambach – Climbing partner on the Summit America expedition and co-record holder of fifty U.S. highpoints.

Be inspired for a lifetime! Todd will inspire your audience to overcome their challenges and achieve their goals and dreams. He has successfully spoken internationally to all types and ages of audiences for over 20 years. Your audience will immediately respond to Todd's message and begin making positive changes in their personal and professional lives. Todd often gets stopped by people who have heard him over a decade ago and mention how his story changed their life. Needing a speaker with a powerful and lasting message? Book Todd!

Millions have been inspired by Todd's story, as featured in

* Sports Illustrated
* *CBS Year in Sports*
* Forbes
* Robert Schuller's *Hour of Power*
* *Chicken Soup for the Soul – A Second Helping*
* Numerous interviews on ABC, NBC, CBS, CNN, TNN
* Featured on the popular shows Extra and Inside Edition
* Wall Street Journal

Most recently, Todd was honored to be invited as contributor for Huffington Post.

Todd's perseverance in the face of seemingly insurmountable challenges has won him many awards, including:

* Ten Outstanding Young Americans Award
* Henry Iba Award for Outstanding Citizen Athlete
* Class Act Award
* American Red Cross Everyday Hero Award
* Inducted into the Energizer Hall of Fame

Join the thousands who have heard Todd give his "More than Mountains" speech, with its inspirational message and engaging multi-media presentation of his Summit America Expedition, for your business, association, school, civic or religious organization. He works closely with event organizers to understand the challenges facing their audience members so he can tailor his message specifically to meet their current needs: **motivation, leadership, communication, safety, peak performance, teamwork, and more.**

To book Todd for your next event, contact him at
todd@toddhuston.com
(918)978-8633

www.toddhuston.com